I0490307

ART BOOKS

FROM CRESCENT MOON PUBLISHING

Leonardo da Vinci
by James Pearson

Early Netherlandish Painting
by Rosalind Mutter

Piero della Francesca
by Naomi Haskell

Giovanni Bellini
by Julia Davis

Eric Gill: Nuptials of God
by Anthony Hoyland

Minimal Art and Artists In the 1960s and After
by Laura Garrard

Postwar Art
by George Knighton

Vincent van Gogh: Visionary Landscapes
by Stuart Morris

Max Beckmann
by Stuart Morris

Egon Schiele: Sex and Death in Purple Stockings
by D. Simon Eade

Mark Rothko: The Art of Transcendence
by Julia Davis

Jasper Johns
by L.M. Poole

Brice Marden
by Laura Garrard

Frank Stella: American Abstract Artist
by James Pearson

Bellini
By Jennie Ellis Keysor

The Life of Michelangelo Buonarroti
By John Addington Symonds

Dante Gabriel Rossetti
By Esther Wood

Rodin: The Man and His Art
Edited by Judith Cladel

Rodin
By Rainer Maria Rilke

Fra Angelico
By James Mason

The Madonna In Art
By Estelle Hurll

The Venetian School of Painting
By Evelyn Phillipps

Leonardo da Vinci
By Maurice Brockwell

Famous European Painters
By Sarah Bolton

Delacroix
By Paul Konody

BOUCHER

BOUCHER

BY HALDANE MACFALL

CRESCENT MOON

First published 1908. This edition © 2019.

Printed and bound in the U.S.A.
Set in Book Antiqua 10 on 14pt.
Designed by Radiance Graphics.

British Library Cataloguing in Publication data

ISBN-13 978186171716422

CRESCENT MOON PUBLISHING
P.O. Box 1312, Maidstone, Kent, ME14 5XU
Great Britain, www.crmoon.com

CONTENTS

NOTE ON THE TEXT

The text is from *Boucher* by Haldane McFall, published by
Frederick A. Stokes, New York, 1908.

The illustrations discussed in the book are included in the
illustrations section, along with many other works.

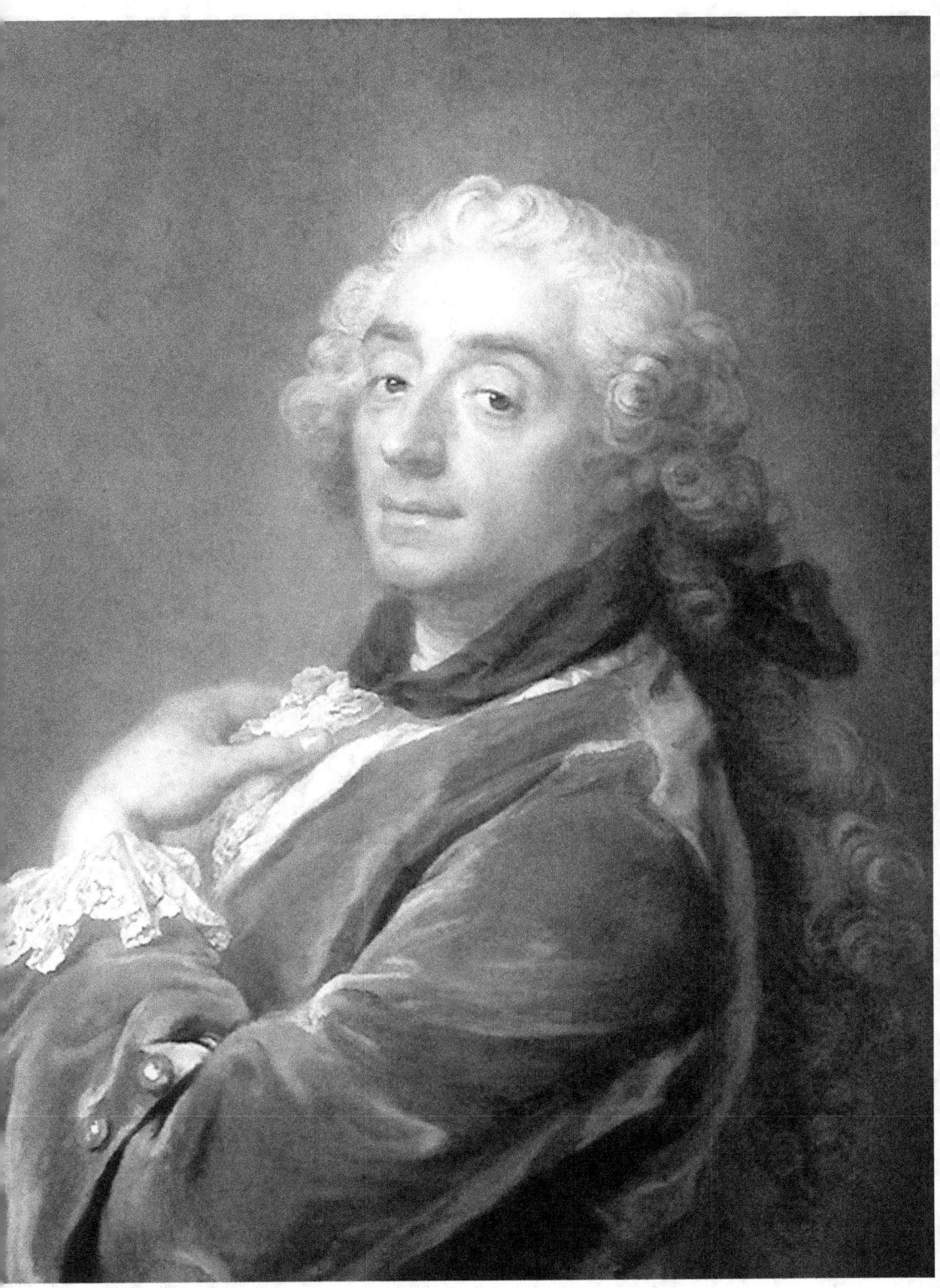

François Boucher by Gustav Lundberg, 1741

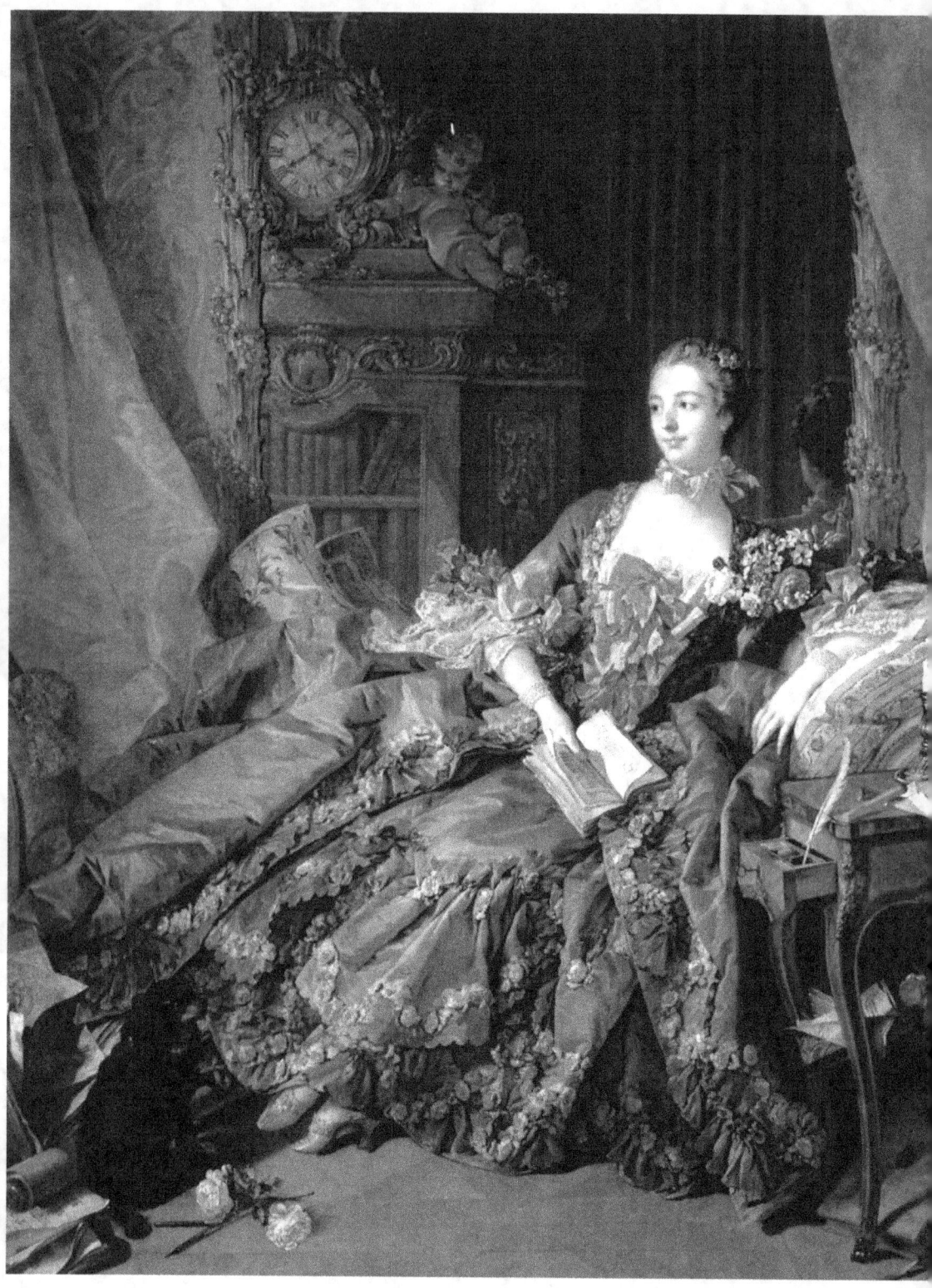

François Boucher, Madame de Pompadour

I

THE SMALL BEGINNINGS

The year after good Queen Anne came to rule over us, Louis the Fourteenth being still King of France, on an autumn day in the October of 1703, that saw the trees of Paris shedding their parched leaves as a carpet to the feet of the much-bewigged dandified folk who stepped it swaggeringly down the walks of the Palais Royal, swinging long canes, and strutting along the shaded promenades of the more fashionable places of the city, there stood in the vestry of the parish church of Saint Jean-en-Grève a little group of the small burgess folk, gathered about a little infant, whilst the tipstaff to the king's palace, one François Prévost, signed solemnly as witness to the birth-certificate and as acknowledged godfather to the aforesaid morsel of humanity, which, as the certificate badly set forth in black and white for ever, was henceforth to be known for good or ill as François Boucher, first-born son, on the 29th of September, four days past, of the tipstaff's friend, Nicolas Boucher, "maître-peintre," who stood hard by, and of his wife Elizabeth Lemesle.

The worthy tipstaff's writing done, he bowed in the best Court manner to Mademoiselle Boullenois, daughter to yonder consequential fellow, the law officer from the Police Court; and handed her the inked quill to bear witness in her turn as godmother.

The sand being flung upon the wet ink, and the blotting done, there was exchange of compliments in the stilted manner of good-fellowship of the day between priest and party – tapping of snuff-boxes and taking of snuff, with more than a little gossip of the Court and some shaking of heads, and under-lips solemnly thrust forth; the gossip is not without authority and weight, for is not godfather Prévost tipstaff to the king's majesty, therefore in the whirl of things?

The child, indeed, was born into a Paris agog with stirring affairs. Well might heads be shaken solemnly. The French arms were knowing defeat. The Englishman, Marlborough, was flinging back the French armies wheresoever he gave them battle. Europe was one great armed camp. France was suffering terrible blood-letting. Defeat came on defeat. These were sorry times. On land all went wrong. Good generals were set aside; intriguing good-for-nothings led the veterans into disaster. But there was still France upon the high seas.

Then the women folk, bored with high politics, would draw back the talk to the infant François, and there would be genial banter about the morsel; for was he not a Saturday child, therefore bound to be a bit of a scamp!

And so, off to Monsieur Boucher's modest little home in the Rue de Verrerie to a glass of wine and further compliments and banter, and more vague surmises as to what lay upon the knees of the gods for little François Boucher.

II

THE STUDENT

Yes, the sun of the Grand Monarque was setting. Louis Quatorze was nearing the end of his long lease of splendour. Our little François was not a month old when Admiral Rooke whipped Château-Renaud off the high seas, destroying the French and Spanish fleets in Vigo Bay, and carrying off some millions of pieces of eight from the galleons as treasure. The child's first year saw the English troopers ride down the French at Blenheim – a day that made "Malbrook" a name of dread to every French child, a name to frighten into good behaviour. To the little fellow's home came the horror-spoken talk of Ramilies; then of Oudenarde; then of Lille – to his six-year-old ears the terrible news of Malplaquet.

But there was Paris a-bellringing in his ears at seven; for there was born to the king's grandson a sickly child that was to succeed him as Louis the Fifteenth. And François Boucher is one day to step from his modest home and stand nearer at this child's side than he thinks.

The boy Boucher, at sturdy twelve, would recall the death of the old king in his lonely last years, and the setting upon the ancient throne of France of the five-year-old child as Louis Quinze

– a comely little fellow – with Orleans as Regent. Young François Boucher was to spend his youth and grow up to manhood in a France that lay under the regency of this dissolute, brilliant Orleans.

Nicolas Boucher, the father, seems to have been an obscure, honest fellow, given to the *trade* of art, and that too in mediocre fashion enough, designing embroideries, covers for chairs, and the like – "an inferior designer, little favoured by fortune," runs the recorded verdict of his day. But he had the virtue of recognising his mediocrity, and the desire to save his son from the sordid cares of mediocre artistry; since, having himself given the boy his schooling with pencil and brush, and brought the lad up in an atmosphere of art and in the company of artists, he had the astuteness to send him to the studio of Lemoyne, a really great painter and rapidly becoming famous – he who painted the ceilings of Versailles with gods and goddesses in handsome fashion.

Lemoyne was a well-chosen master for the promising youth of seventeen. He had founded his art upon that of Correggio and Veronese, had rid himself of hard academic tendencies, and was painting in a sound French fashion. The youth Boucher, with the quick and astounding gift, that he displayed all through his life, of rapidly making his own what he wanted to acquire, picked up from Lemoyne at once a French way of stating what he desired to state, in a large, broad manner, without having to go through the long years of drudgery to Italian models of style which was then the only schooling for an artist – was therefore enabled to free himself from the equally long years that it would have taken him to rid the Italian style from his artistry. In short, the youth of seventeen made Lemoyne's art his own in a few weeks; and, on the eve of manhood, he so rivalled his master in accomplishment that it is dangerous to attribute a picture of this time to the master or the pupil without most careful evidence.

Yet the youth vowed that he was but three months with Lemoyne, who, said he, took scant interest in his pupils. But it must be remembered that Boucher was a prodigious worker, with a passionate love for his work that lasted until death took the brush from his fingers, and that he had a quick and alert mind and hand, free from the hesitances of a student, and always daring in experiment. To wish to achieve a thing, for Boucher, was to set him to its achievement. He rested neither night nor day until he mastered that which he had set out to do. On the day he left Lemoyne's studio he stepped out of it a finished artist, a sound painter, fully equipped with all the craftmanship, trade-secrets, and tricks of thumb that it had taken his master his life to learn – and a facile copyist of his style and handling. It was the sincerest form of flattery; and Boucher, to the end of his days, held the art of Lemoyne in the greatest reverence – as is proved by his answer, when at the very height of his fame, to one who asked him to complete a picture by his master: "Such works are to me sacred vessels," said he – "I should dread to profane them by touching them."

Lemoyne's admiration for his pupil was not lacking in return. The youth painted, whilst with his master, a picture of a "Judgment of Susanna," before which Lemoyne stood astounded, then burst into prophecy of Boucher achieving greatness in the years to come.

From Lemoyne's studio, the young fellow went to live with "Père Cars," the engraver, whose son, Laurent, was a friend of the youth, and who engaged him to design the drawings for his engravers, allowing him in return his food, lodging, and sixty livres (double-florins) a month – some twelve pounds. Boucher accounted his fortune made.

The cheery youth went at his work with energy and enthusiasm, blithely setting his hand to anything that was wanted of him, bringing charm and invention to all he did – tailpieces, frontispieces, emblems, coats of arms, freemason's certificates, first-communion cards, initial letters. He was soon set to work upon important designs for engravings. He searched out the publishers of books, and let no chance escape of working for them.

Thus and otherwise he filled his scanty purse – that needed filling, for he was quick at its emptying, being of a free hand and generous disposition. And hard as he worked, so did he play. Work and pleasure were his joy in life.

And all the time he was taking part in the students' competitions for the Academy.

It was in his nineteenth year that, in this same Paris, in the house of one of its rich families, was born a little girl-child who was to come into Boucher's life in after years. The father, a financial fellow, one Poisson, was a man of shady repute; indeed he was under banishment for mis-handling the public moneys at the time of the birth of the little girl-child, christened Jeanne Antoinette Poisson – destined to be the Jane of the scurrilous street songs of the years to come. But the careless student knew little of it as yet, nor that destiny had put into the pretty child's cradle the sceptre and diadem of France as plaything.

Boucher, on the eve of manhood, took as little heed of the child's coming as did the thirteen-year-old lad who sat upon the throne, and who, in little Jane Poisson's first year, was declared to be of man's estate and ruler of France, no longer requiring Regent Orleans to govern for him.

It was in this his nineteenth year that Boucher took the first prize at the Academy with his picture of "Evilmerodach, son and successor of Nebuchadnezzar, delivering Joachin from chains, in which his father had for a long time held him."

This success set the collectors buying pictures by the brilliant youngster. But François Boucher needs no paying orders to make him work – he paints for the love of the thing, declares that his "studio is his church," and seeks to display his art and spread the repute of it abroad. And his fame grows apace, if at a cost. Nay, he courts fame even to the extent of hanging his pictures upon the tapestries and carpets and such like draperies that the police oblige the citizens to hang out from their houses along the Place Dauphin and the Pont-Neuf during the procession of the Fête-

Dieu – called the *Exposition de la Jeunesse.*

There was a thing happened about this time that was to be of large significance to the young fellow's craftsmanship. Watteau had lately died, his eager will burning out the poor stricken body. His friend De Julienne, anxious to publish a book to Watteau's memory, strolled into the engraving-studio behind "Père Cars'" shop, where Boucher and his comrade, Laurent Cars, were wont to spend a part of their time; and he commissioned Boucher to engrave 125 of the plates after the dead master. Watteau's essentially French influence was the impulse above all others to thrust forward the development of Boucher's genius along its right path, and sent his art towards its great goal. The business was a rare delight to the young artist, and in the doing of it he learnt many lessons which added greatly to the enhancement of his style; whilst the payment of twenty-four livres (double-florins) a day still further increased his delight and contentment.

He completed the series with his wonted fiery zeal and rapid facility, and thus and otherwise, hotly pursuing his study of nature and his art, he arrived at the moment when his education should receive its inevitable finishing state in the Italian tour; so to Rome he went with Carle Van Loo and his two nephews, François and Louis Van Loo.

Of Boucher's wander-years in Italy little is known. He seems to have shown scant respect for the accepted standards of the schools and the critics, to have found Michael Angelo "contorted," Raphael "insipid," and Carrache "gloomy." He, in fact, was drawn only to such artists as were to his taste, and he had the courage to say so. However, whether he were kept idle from ill-health or not; whether his stay were short or not, he appears again in Paris in three years – suspiciously like the three years' conventional Italian study of a first-prize winner of the Academy – with a large number of religious pictures to his credit – pictures that were hailed by the Academicians and critics alike for their beauty, their force, and their virility – pictures which, perhaps fortunately for Boucher's repute, have vanished, or hang in galleries under other names.

Here we see Boucher grimly putting aside his own taste and aims in art, and doggedly bending his will and hand to a prodigious effort to win the reputation and standing of a "serious painter," without which he could not hope to attain academic honours. He won them; for, in this his twenty-eighth year, on his return to Paris, he was "nominated" to the Academy. He had but to present an Historical Painting in order to take his seat as an Academician.

III

VENUS AND MARRIAGE

Back in his beloved Paris again; thrilled by the atmosphere and gaiety of its merry life; in the full vigour of manhood on the eve of his thirties; amongst congenial friends; done with the drudgery of winning to Academic honour, Boucher saw that the public were not falling over each other to purchase religious or historic pictures; he straightway turned his back upon these things, and on the edge of his thirtieth year he gave to the world his "Marriage of the Children of God with the Children of Men," in which Venus is the avowed mistress of his adoration. It caused a fine stir, and greatly increased his repute.

In this picture he ends his Italian period and strikes his own personal note. Both this and the "Venus asking arms for Aeneas from Vulcan," together with the "Birth of Adonis" and the "Death of Adonis," of about the same period, still show Boucher strongly under the influence of his master, Lemoyne. Indeed, the "Birth" and "Death of Adonis," their record lost during the scuffle and confusion of the Revolution, for long hung side by side as pictures by Lemoyne, until, being cleaned about 1860, Boucher's initials were discovered upon them, and, contemporary engravings being hunted up, still further proved their origin. But in the

Venus that now figures in all his works there is that flesh-painting of the nude, and that rosy touch upon the flesh of the female figure, that are a far more certain signature of Boucher's handiwork than any written name.

Unfortunately the Salons were closed during Boucher's earlier years until he was thirty-four, and the record of his work during these years is difficult to follow; but with his service to Venus his personal career begins, and the stream of his Venus-pieces steadily flows from his hands.

He came to her service rid of all prentice essays in craftsmanship, a finished and consummate artist. He found in his subject a goddess to whom he could devote his great and splendid gifts. He painted her dainty body with a radiant delight and a rare colour-sense such as France had never before seen or uttered. He remains to this day the first painter of the subtle, delicate, and elusive thing that is femininity; he caught her allure, her charm, as he was to catch the fragrance and charm of children and flowers; and he set the statement of these things upon canvas as they have never been uttered.

The whole of his life long, Boucher gave himself up with equal and passionate devotion to work and to pleasure – working at his easel often twelve hours of his day without losing, to the end when the brush fell from his dead fingers, his blitheness of heart or his generosity of act, and without weakening the pleasure-loving desires of his gadding spirit. Out of his splendid toil he made the means to indulge his tastes for pleasure; and the gratifying of his tastes in turn renewed and created the ideas that made the subjects of his artistry. He brought to all he did a joy in the doing that made of his vast labour one long pleasure – of his pleasures a riot of industry. He played as he toiled, scarce knowing which was play and which toil.

The gossip of his love-affairs makes no romantic story – they were but commonplace ecstasies with unknown frail women. But hard as he worked and lived and played, he found time to get himself married in his thirtieth year to pretty seventeen-year-old

Marie Jeanne Buseau, a little Parisian – and for love of her, so far as he understood the business; for she brought him no dowry.

The young couple settled down for the next ten years in the Rue Saint-Thomas-du-Louvre. Here Boucher lived through his thirties.

Madame was a pretty creature, if we had but Latour's pastel portrait alone to prove it. But the pretty features were the crown to as pretty a body, for she sat often to her lord; and it is clear from his correspondence with a friend, Bachaumont, that she is the Psyche of his illustrated fable – and Psyche runs much to the Altogether. Marriage, however, was not likely to imprison Boucher's gadding eyes; and it did not. Madame Boucher seems to have had as frail a heart, and avoided strife by amusing herself, amongst others, with the Swedish Ambassador, Count de Tessin, who, to gain access to the lady, commissioned Boucher to do the Watteau-like illustrations to *Acajou* – a dull affair. Boucher's pretty wife, herself no mean artist, worked in his studio, and painted several smaller canvases after his pictures, gaining some fame as a miniaturist and engraver.

Nor did Marriage turn Boucher from his art. Two years were gone by since his nomination to the Academy; he had now to paint the formal Historical Picture and present it in order to take his seat as Academician; and it was in this his thirtieth year that he painted and won his academic rank with the "Renauld et Armide" now at the Louvre. Here he sufficiently subordinated his own style to the academic to ensure success; and the work was hailed by Academicians and critics, including Diderot, with enthusiasm. But even here we have his cupids peeping round the mythologic event; and Armide herself has pretty French lips that knew no Greek.

Once secure of his position, he straightway flung the last remnants of the academic style out of his studio door; and it is a grim comment on criticism that it was just exactly in proportion as he developed his own personal genius and uttered the France of his day, that he was attacked; whilst the stilted things that he knew were third-rate, and which he wholly rejected from henceforth, were exactly the things that were praised!

His election to the Academy, and the enthusiasm over the picture that won him his seat thereat, brought his name before the young king; the following year he received his first order from the Court whose painter he was destined to become. The decorations in the queen's apartments were gloomy and had grown black; and he painted in their stead the "Charity," "Abundance," "Fidelity," and "Prudence" still there to be seen. Indeed, with his gay vision, his pretty habit of culling only the flowers from the garden of life, and his quickness to set down the pleasing thing in every prospect, Boucher was the destined painter of a Court weary of pomposity and the pose of the mock-heroic, and which was wholly giving itself up to pleasure and the elegances.

But neither his new dignity of Academician nor the royal favour, kept him from the bookshops; and he illustrated, with rare beauty and a charm worthy of Watteau, the great edition of the *Works of Molière* in his thirty-first year. It is true that he made as free with Molière's world as with the Gods of Olympus; he peoples the plays with characters of his own day, arrayed in the dress and habit of that day, and moving in surroundings that he saw about him.

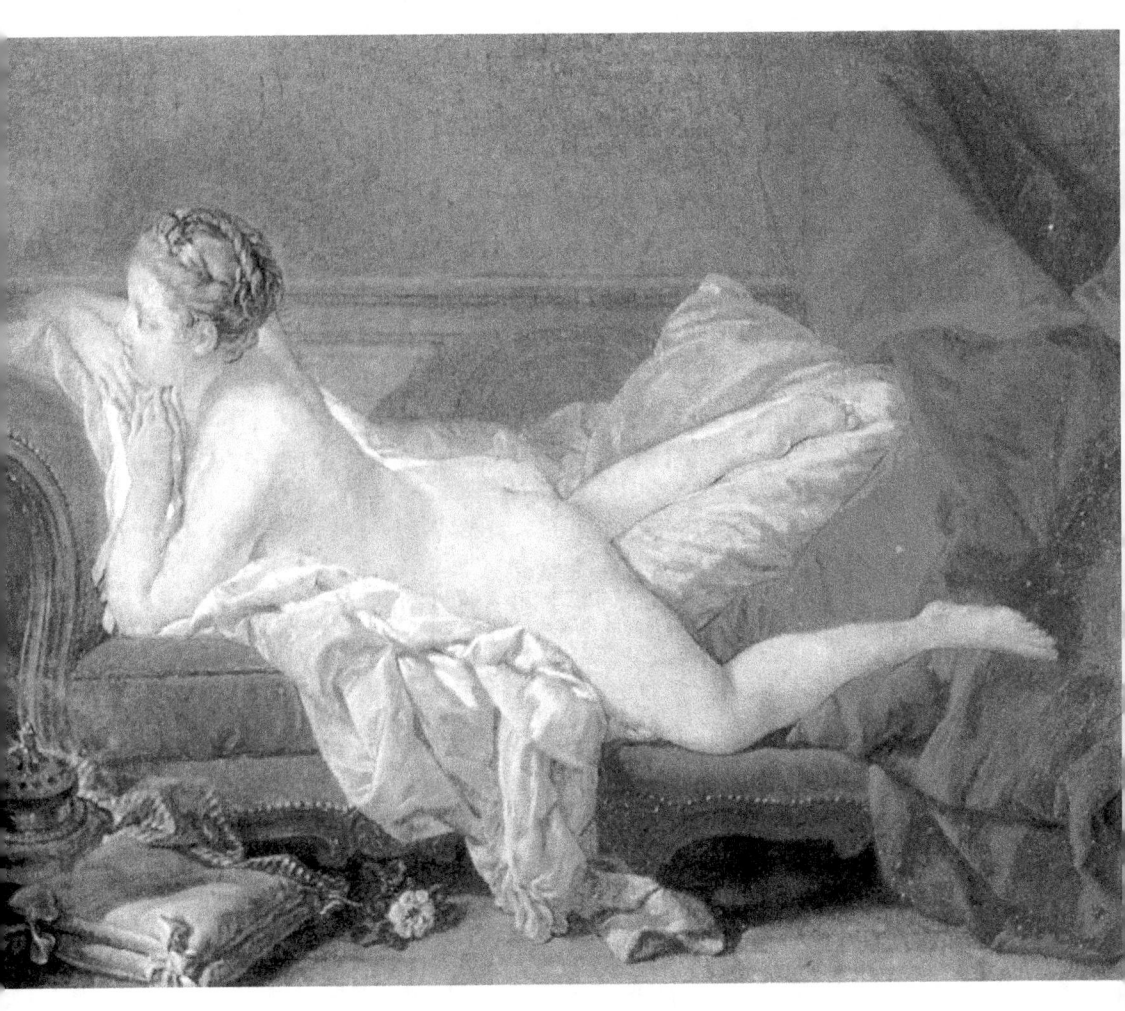

François Boucher, Madamoiselle O'Murphy, 1751

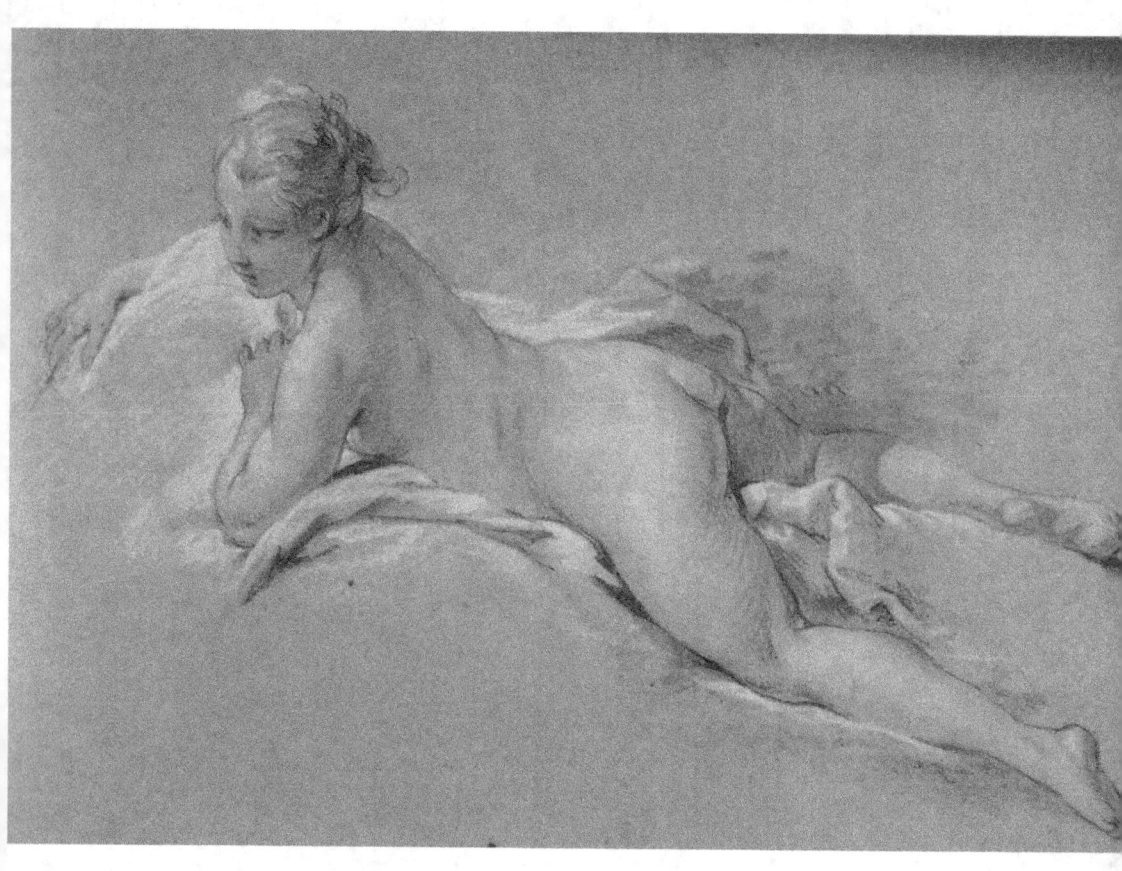

François Boucher

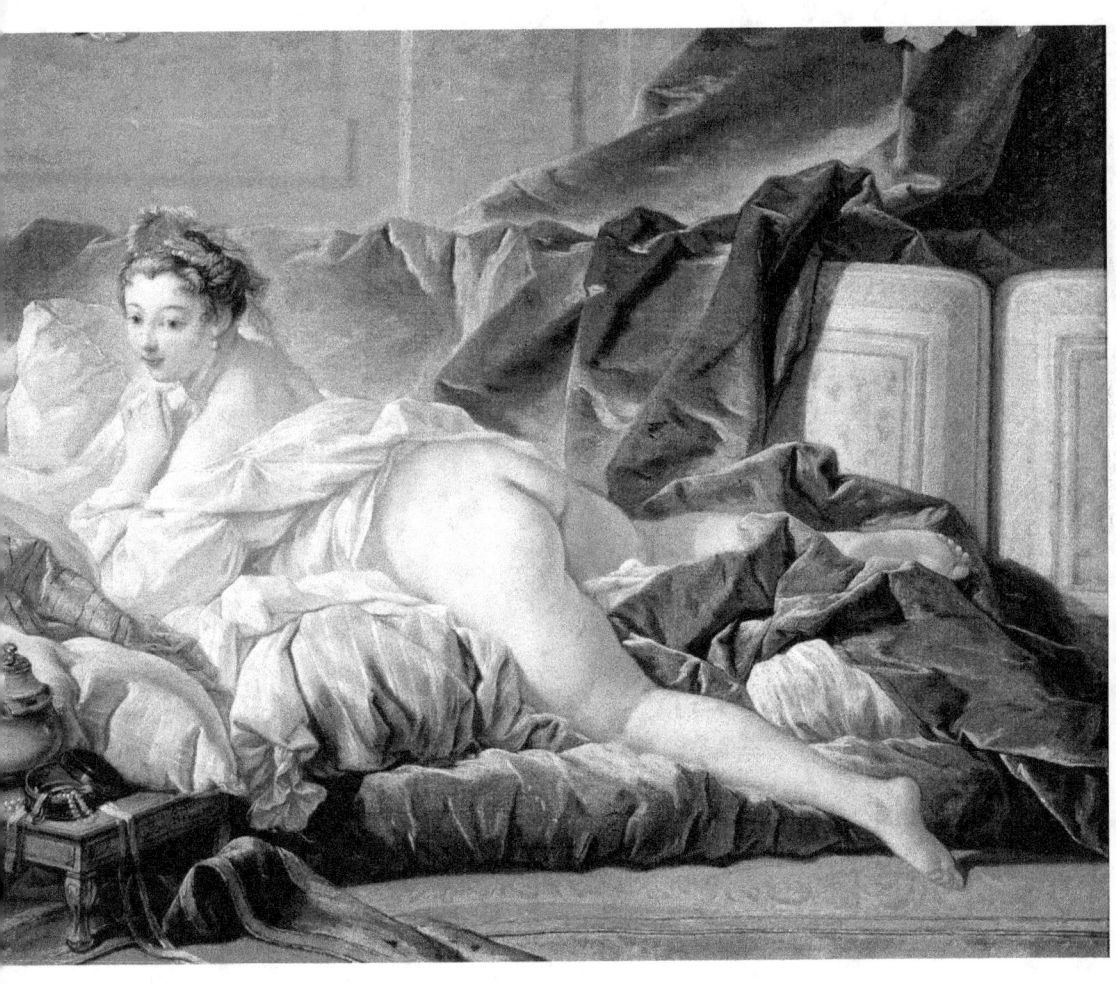

François Boucher, Brown Odalisque

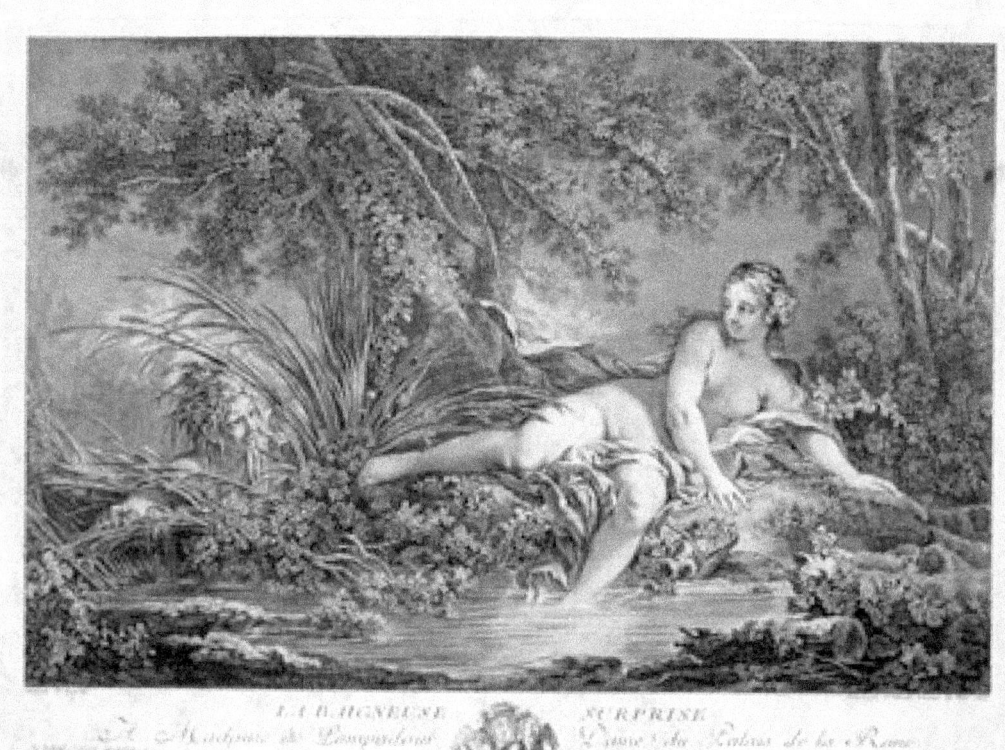

François Boucher, La Baigneuse Surprise

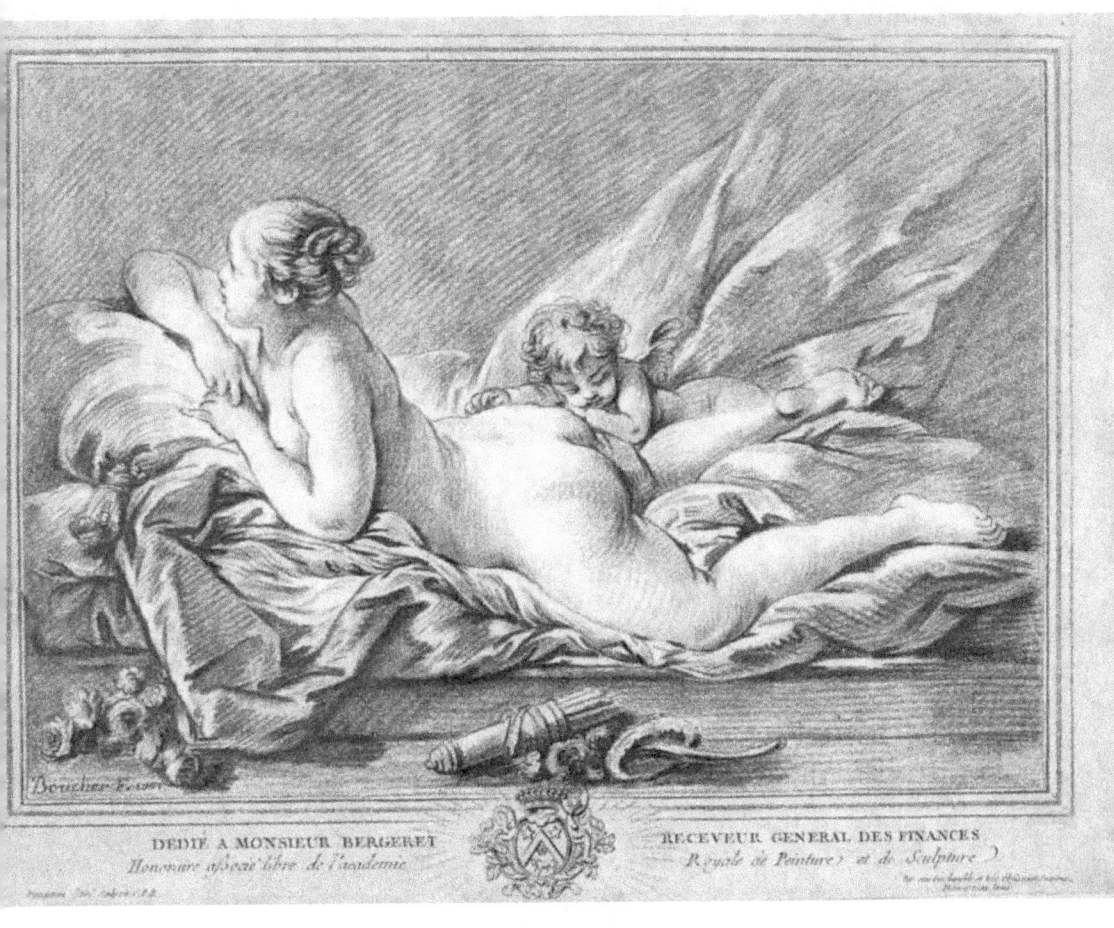

After François Boucher

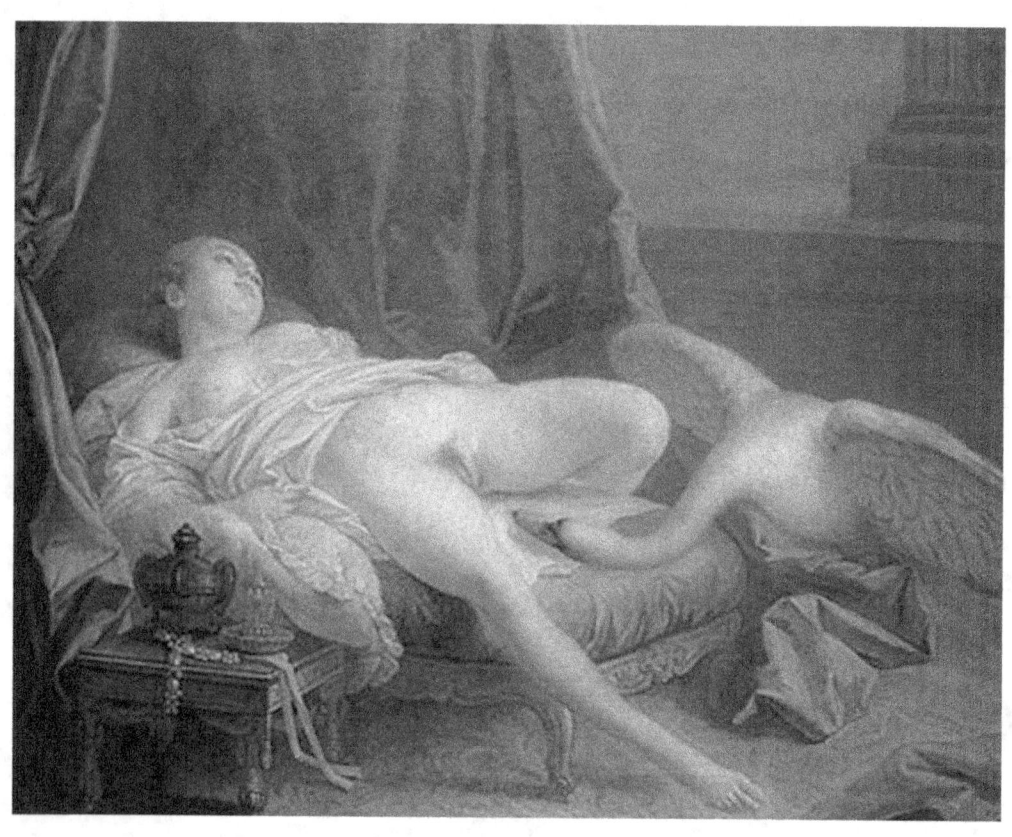

François Boucher, Leda and the Swan

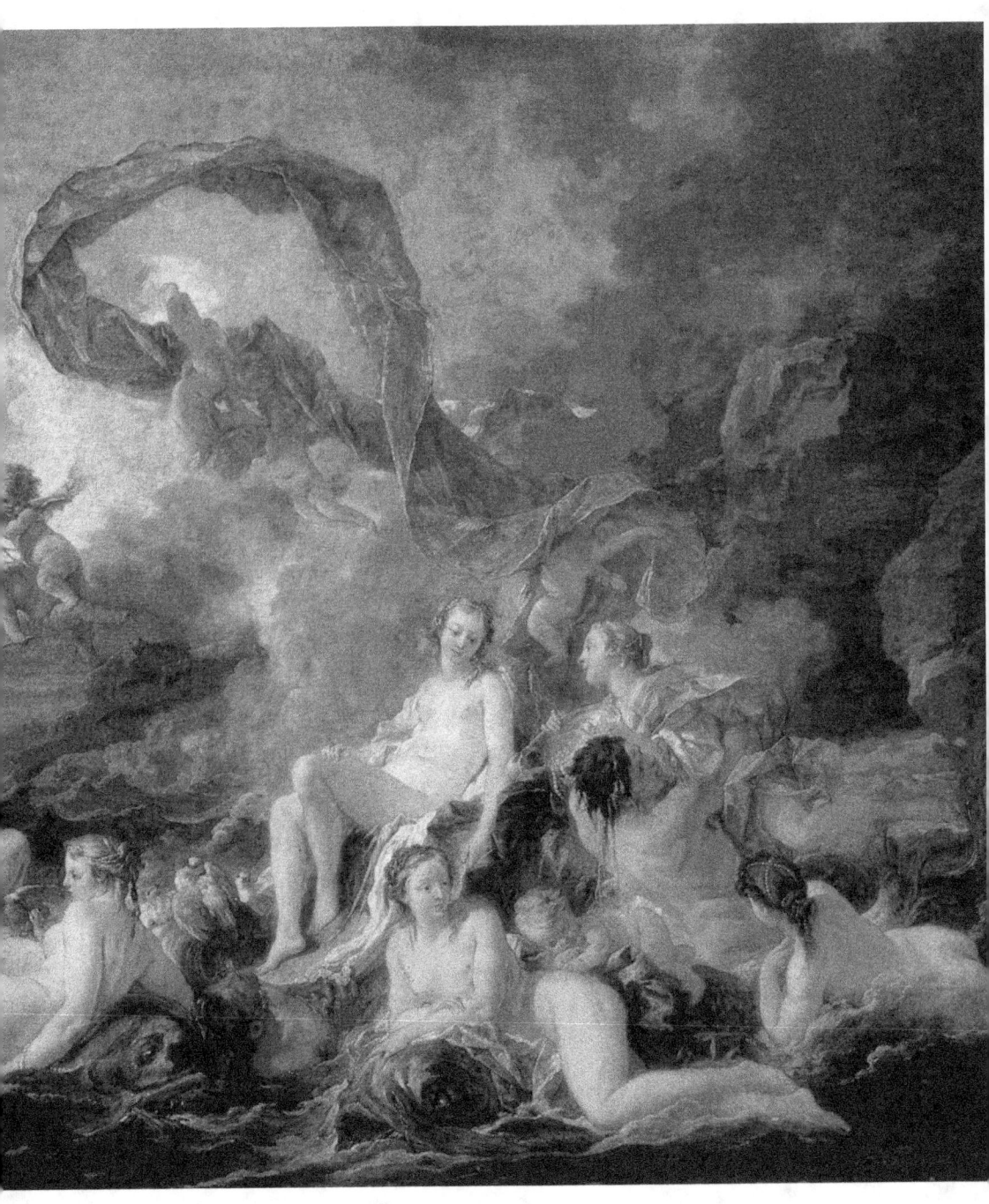

François Boucher, Venus Triumphant, 1740

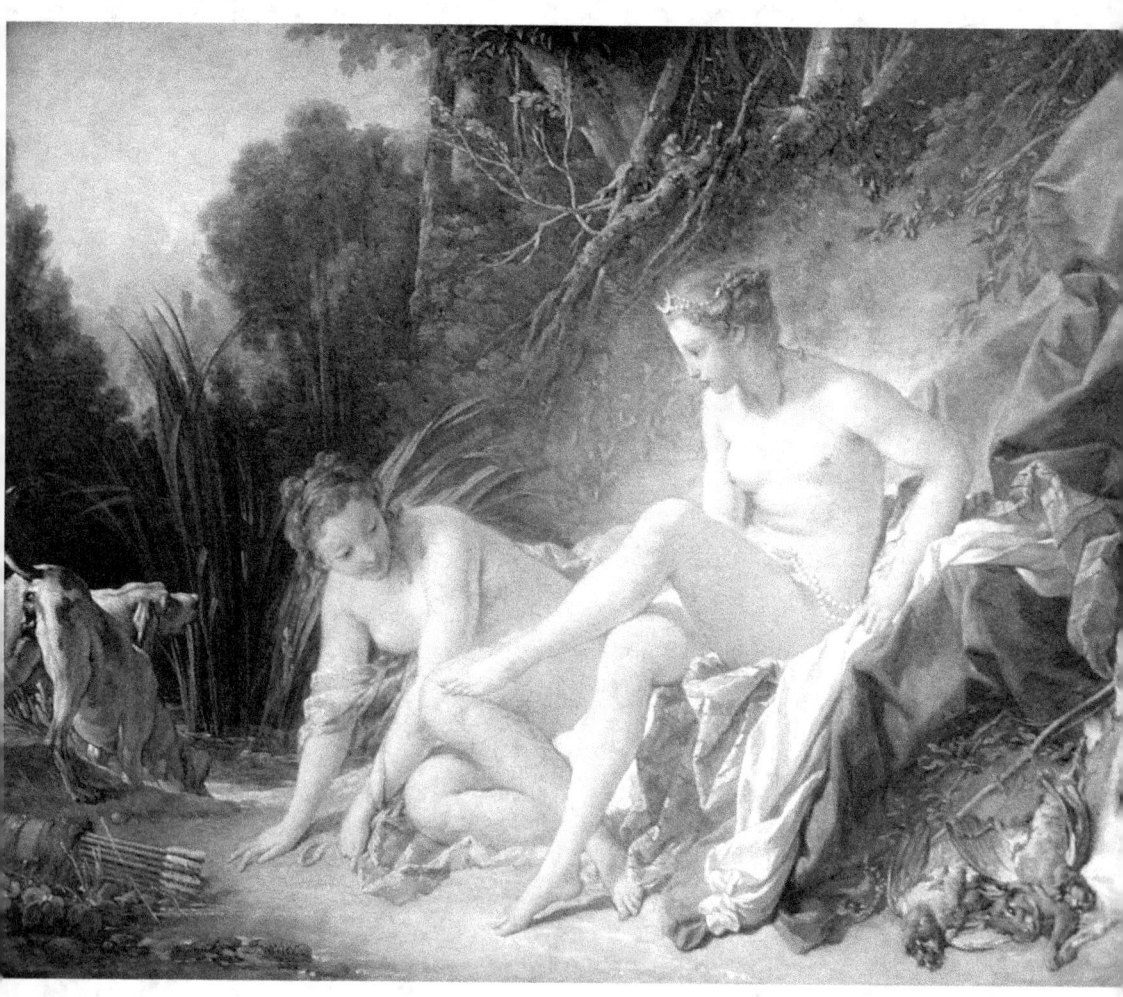

François Boucher, Diana, Louvre, Paris

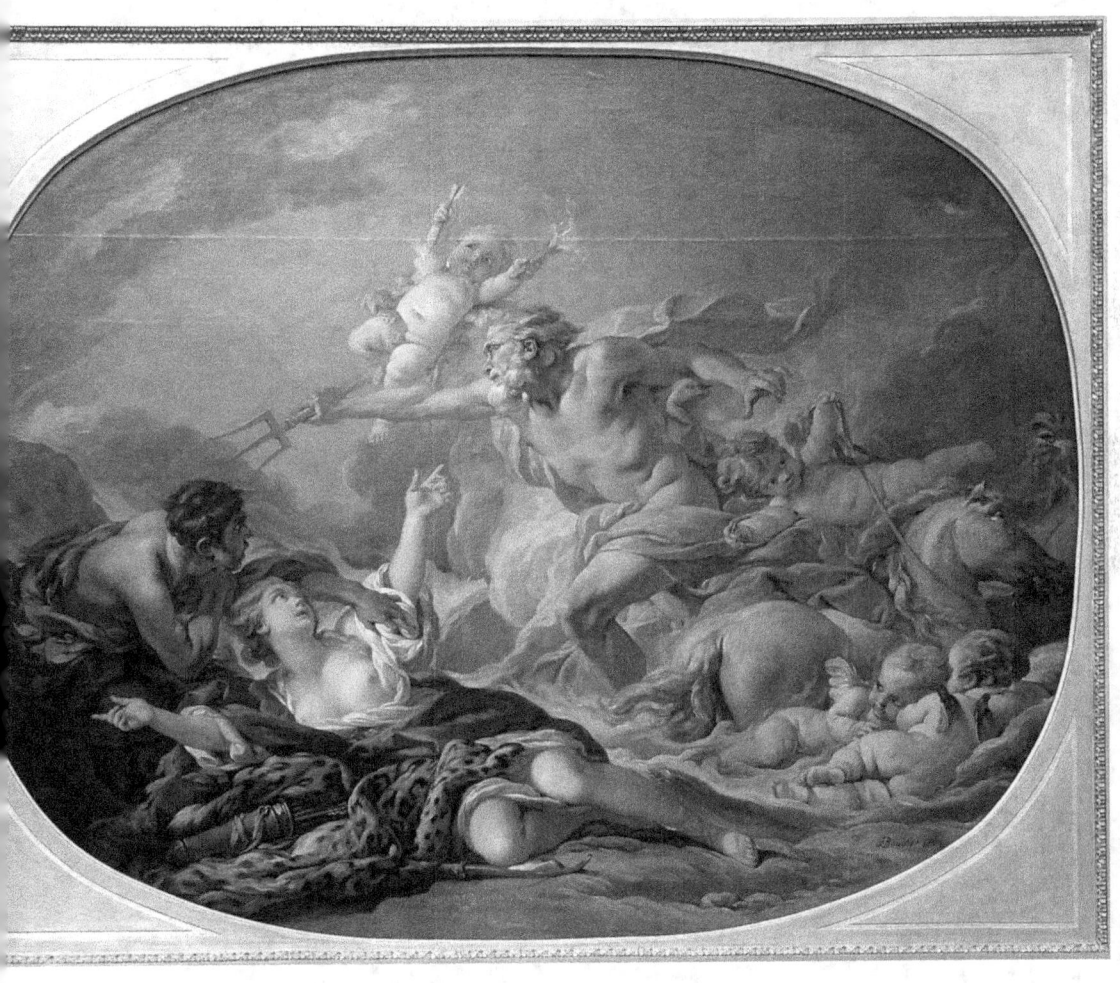

François Boucher, Neptune and Amymone, 1764, Rennes

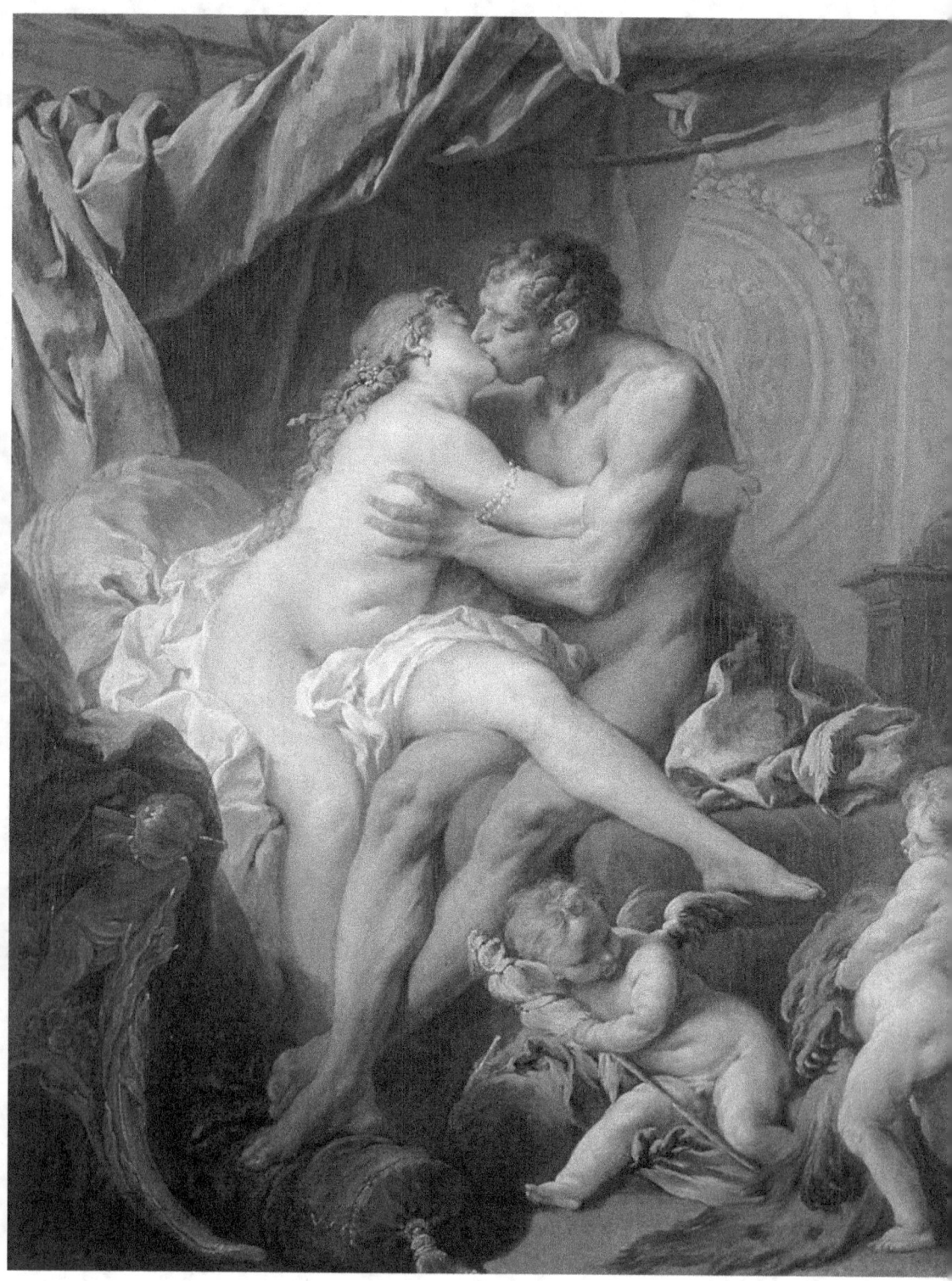

François Boucher, Hercules and Omphale

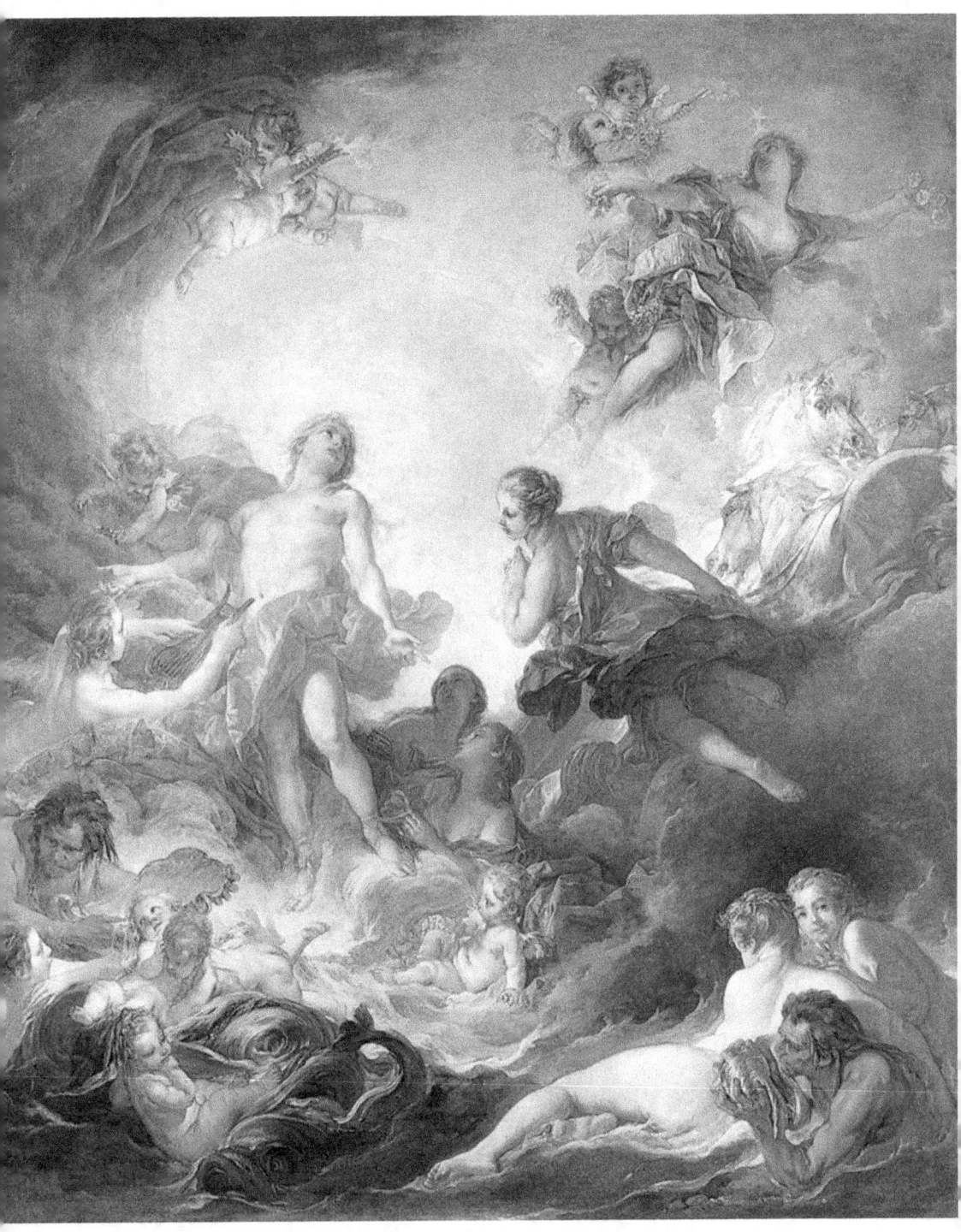

François Boucher, Lever du soleil, Wallace Collection, London

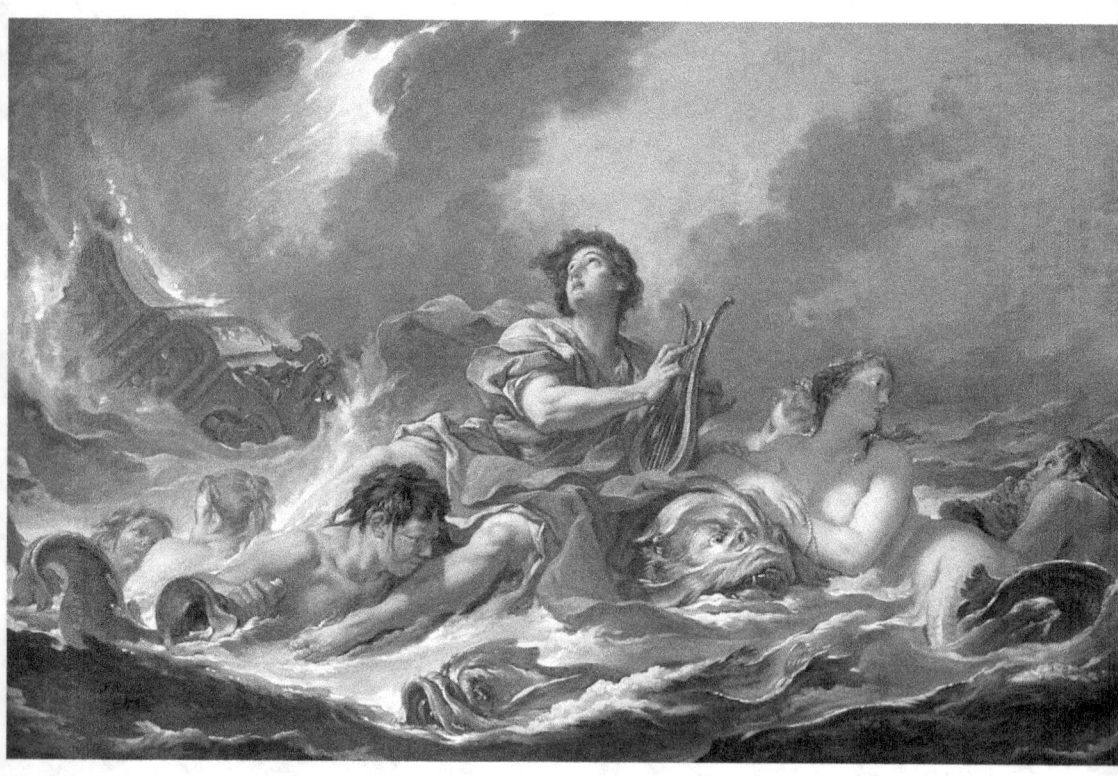

François Boucher, Arion On the Dolphin, 1748

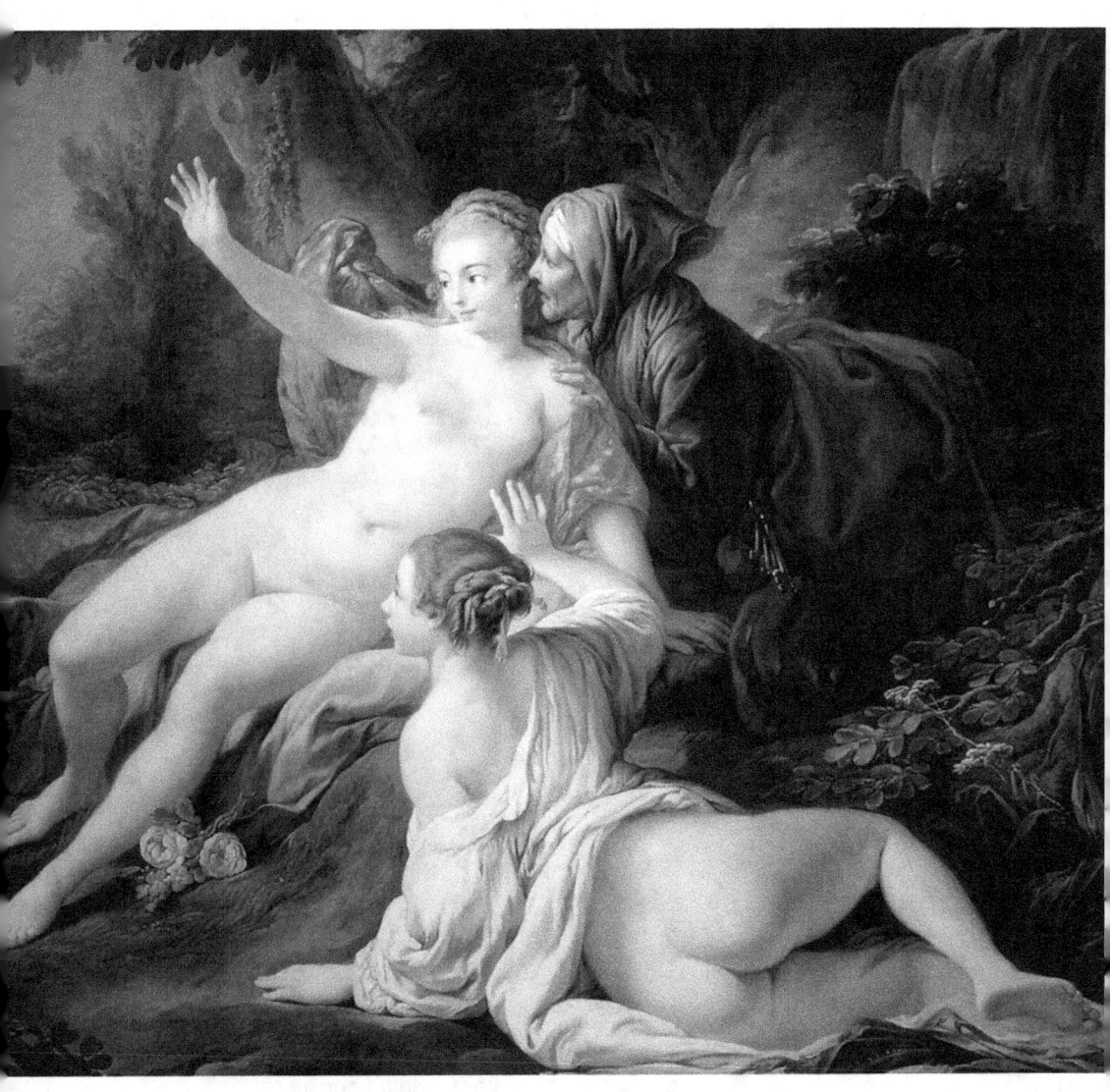

François Boucher, Vertumnus and Pomona, 1740

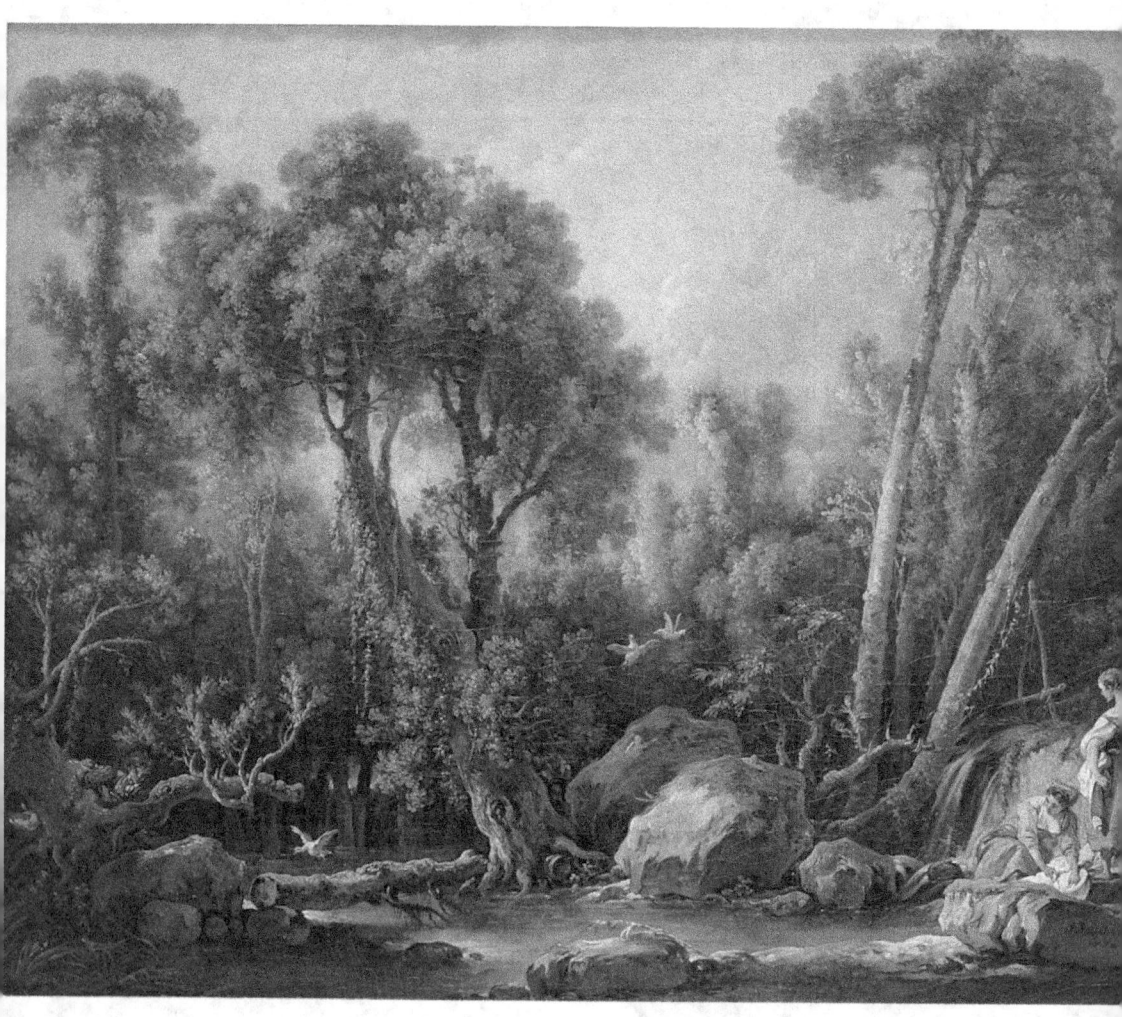

François Boucher, Laundresses In a Landscape

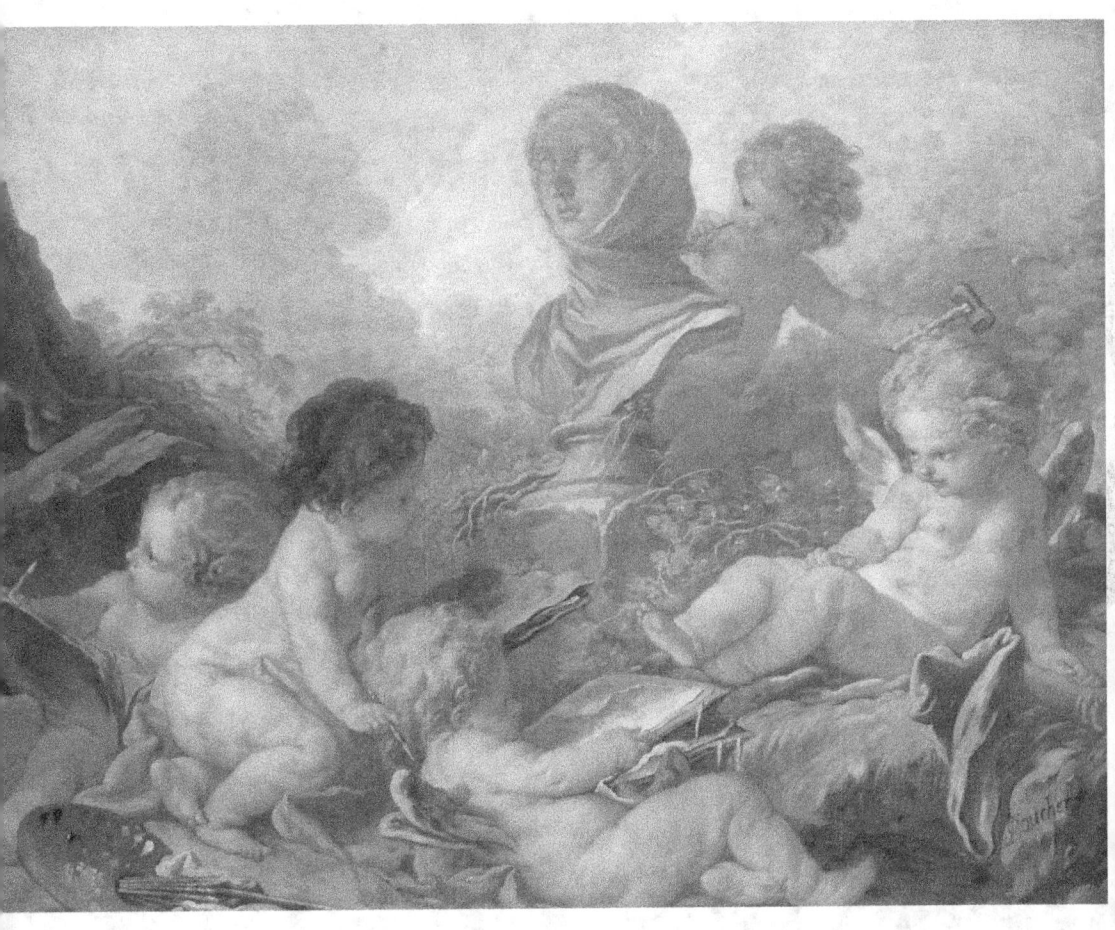

François Boucher, Les Génies des Beaux-Arts

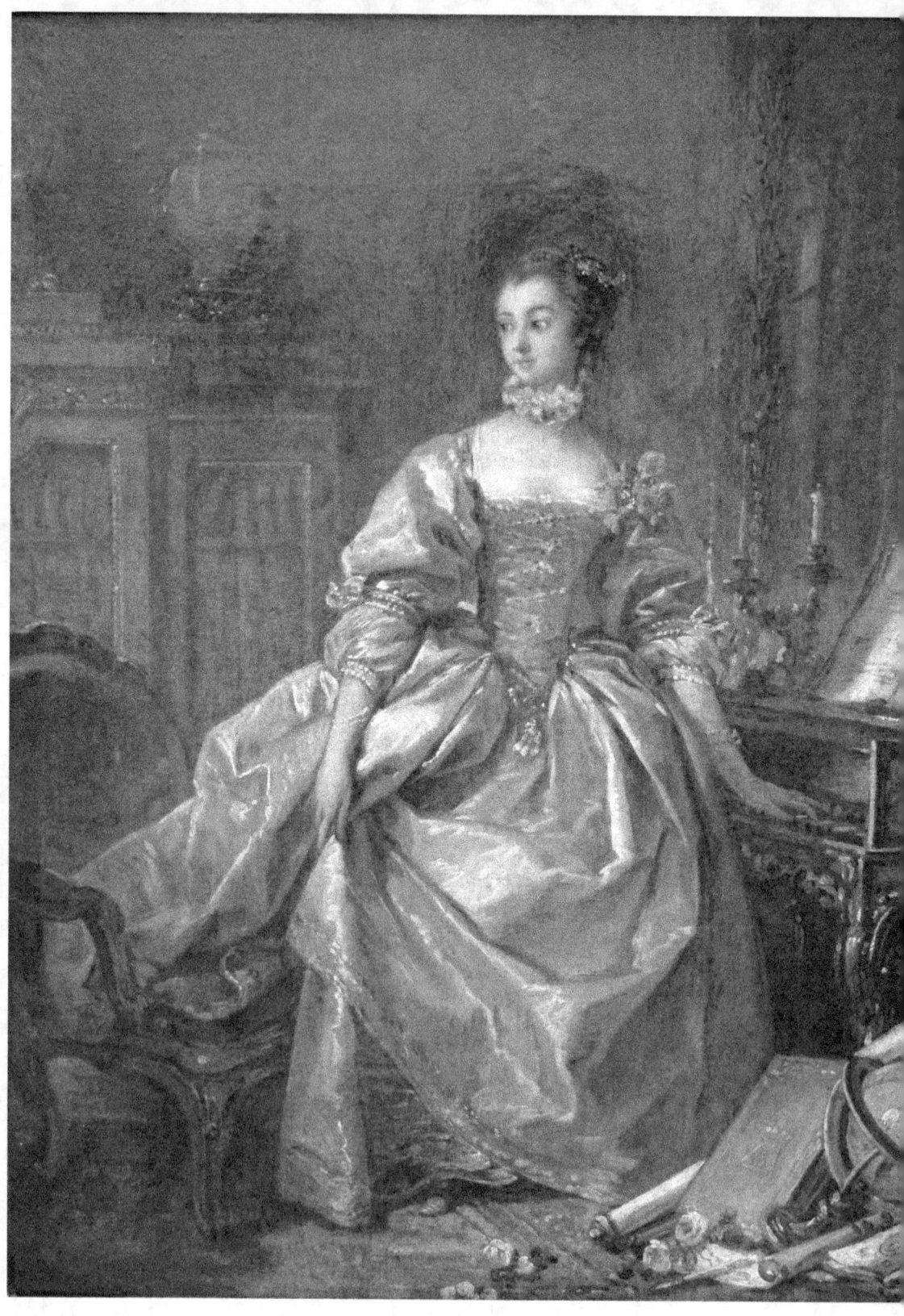

François Boucher, La Marquise de Pompadour

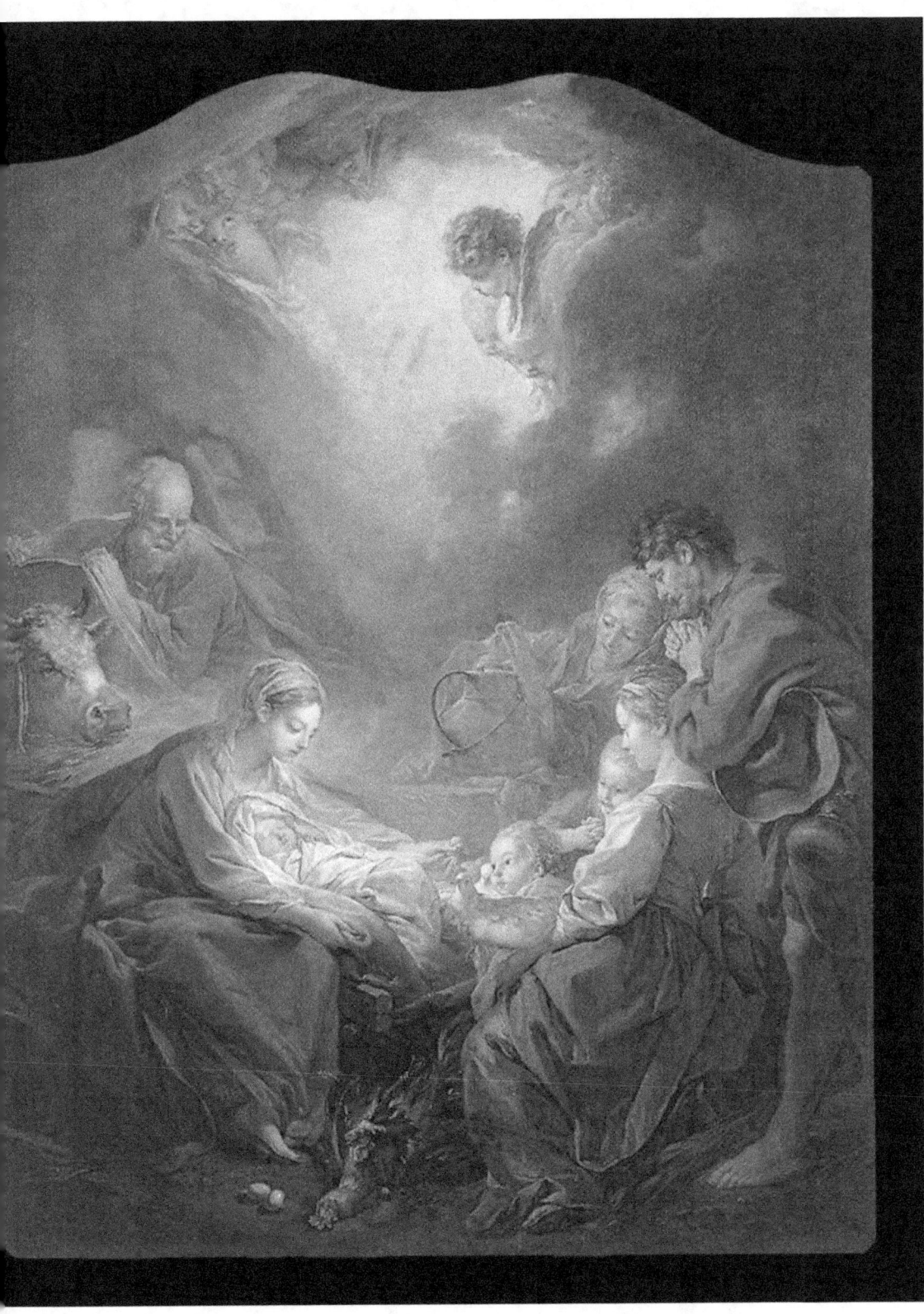

François Boucher, La Lumière du monde

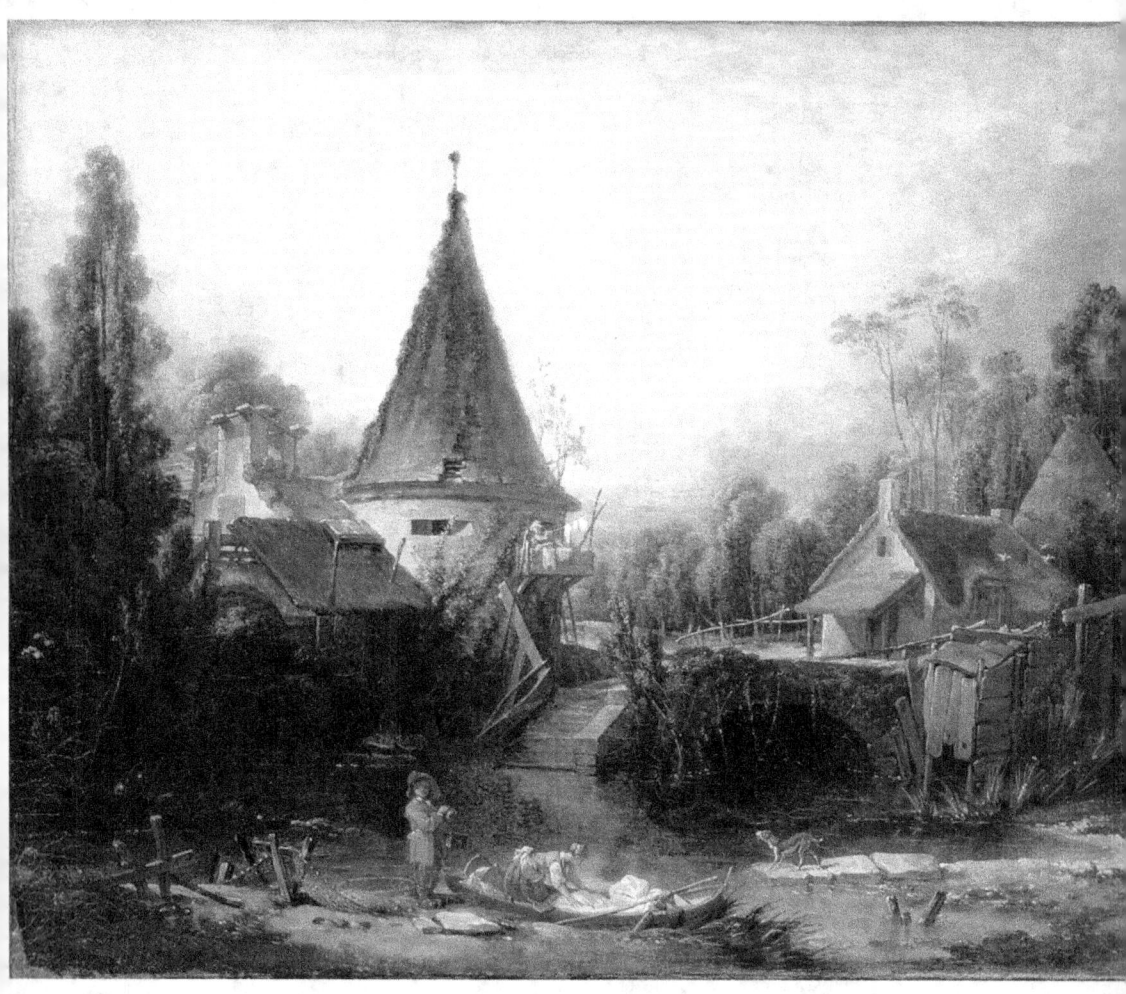

François Boucher, Landscape Near Beauvais

IV

LE MONDE QUI S'AMUSE

The Homely had come upon the town out of Holland, painted with most consummate artistry by Chardin, and was soon in the vogue. Boucher had a quick eye for the mode. And he straightway set himself to the painting of "La Belle Cuisinière." Still-life and homely subjects need an accuracy of realism and a Dutch sense of these things, a sense of sincerity and an appreciation of the dignity of the work-a-day life of the people, in which Boucher was wholly lacking. Above all, it calls for a sense of "character," which, in Boucher, was always weak. It was a sneer against him that his very broomsticks called for pompons and ribbons – and there was more than a little truth in the spite. He is more concerned with the accident of the kissing of a kitchen-maid than with the kitchen's habit. He cannot even peep into a scullery without dragging in Venus by the skirts, and tricking her out in a property-wardrobe of a scullery-wench, in which the girl is clearly but acting the part.

However, these passing vogues and experiments in different methods were only gay asides – he was working the while upon his own subjects; and, to the display by its several members ordered by the Academy, he sent four little paintings of fauns and cupids which won him the honour of election as deputy-professor. His brain and hand were very busy, and he turns from one thing to another with amazing facility, bringing distinction to all that he does.

But he painted about this time two pictures of infants, "L'Amour Oiseleur" and "L'Amour Moissonneur," which were the beginning of that host of cupids that he let fly from his studio; they frolic across his canvases and join the retinue of Venus, peeping out from clouds, over waves, round curtains, painted with a perfection that has never been surpassed in the portrayal of infants. He painted their round limbs, their lusty life, their delightful awkwardnesses, their jolly fat grace, their naïve surprise at life and glory in it, as they had never been painted before, and have never been painted since.

He also gave forth in this his thirty-third year a "Pastoral" and a "Shepherd and Shepherdess in Conversation," with sheep about them and in a pleasant landscape, which were his first essays in the style that he created and which made him famous.

His friend Meissonnier, the inventor of the rococo, stood godfather to Boucher's first-born son in the May of 1736.

From the very beginning Boucher seems to have been engraved. And these engravings, done by the best gravers of his day, greatly extended his reputation and popularised him; he fully realised the value of the advertisement as well as his profits from it. Before his thirty-third year was run out he published his well-known "Cries of Paris." Boucher's description of them, "studies from the low classes," holds the key to that something of failure to realise the dramatic verities that is over all; it gives also the attitude of the France that he knew towards the France that he did not, and could not understand. He created that dainty, pleasant atmosphere that comes floating up to the windows on a fresh morning in Paris from the musical cries of the street vendors; but of the deeper significance of the street-sellers – of the miserable accent in their life, of their weary toil, of the dignity of their labour – he knew nothing; his brush could not refrain from making elegance and fine manners peep from behind the street-porter's fustian or the milkmaid's skirt.

But his thirty-third year was to contain a more far-reaching significance even than the creation of his cupid-pieces and pastorals. The "Cries of Paris" were scarce printed when Boucher's illustration to "Don Quixote" appeared – "Sancho pursued by the servants of the Duke." This design was to have far-reaching results that Boucher little suspected.

The painter Oudry had been called to the conduct of the great tapestry looms at Beauvais a couple of years before; and in his efforts to furnish the looms with good designs, he now called Boucher to his aid, whose original and fresh style, colour, and arrangement, together with his personal vision, and the enthusiasm and zeal with which he threw himself into the work, at once increased the reputation and the products of the famous looms. This large designing for the tapestries was, in return, of immense value to the development of the genius of the man, enlarging his breadth of style and giving scope to that great decorative sense that was his superb gift. Thenceforth he was destined to play a supreme part in the history of the world-famed factories. He now produced painting after painting for the Beauvais looms.

Life is now one long triumph for Boucher, only disturbed in this year by the sad news of the suicide of his old master, Lemoyne. It was in this, Boucher's thirty-fourth year, that the Salon was opened for the first time since Boucher's infancy, and he contributed several canvases to it.

Rigaud, the old Academician, now close upon eighty, straggling through the great galleries, might well blink and gasp at the change that had come over French art since he last exhibited there, thirty-three years gone by; but his scoffs and regrets held no terrors for the younger Academicians gathered about. He stood in a new world. A new generation was in possession. The grand manner, the severe etiquette, formal mock-heroics, and solemn pomposity of Louis the Fourteenth were vanished, and the Agreeable and the Pleasant Make-Believe of Louis the Fifteenth reigned in their stead. Old Rigaud might blink indeed! Just as the imposing and stilted etiquette of the reception-room had given place to the easy manners and airy etiquette of the dainty boudoir, so had light chatter and gay wit and the quick repartee usurped the heavy splendours of a consequential age. France, weary of an eternal pose of the grand manner, was seeking change in joyousness and amusement. Gallantry and gaiety were become the object of the ambition of a dandified and elegant day. France became a coquette; dressed herself as a porcelain shepherdess; and with beribboned crook and sheep, seeking pleasant prospects to stroll through, gave herself to dalliance – her powder-puff and patch-box and fan a serious part of her unseriousness.

V

THE CHÂTEAUROUX

At thirty-five Boucher has arrived. He is in the vogue; in favour at Court – as well as in the fashion. In his three years from taking his seat at the Academy to the opening of the first Salon he has created a new and original style – his cupid pieces, his pastorals, his Venus-pieces, his tapestry. Boucher's kingdom lay in the realm of the decorative painter – and he has found it. Torn from the surroundings for which he designed them, as part and parcel of the general scheme, his pictures are as out of place as an Italian altarpiece in an English dining-room, yet they suffer less. Several may still be seen, as he set them up in frames of his own planning, as overdoors in the palace of the Soubise, now given up to the national archives.

The ghost of the Prince of Soubise, who commissioned them, may haunt his palace, but his kin know the place no longer. The overdoors wrought by Boucher's skill look down now on the nation's collection of historic documents. The "Three Graces enchaining Love," the fine pastoral of "The Cage," and the pastoral of the "Shepherd placing a Rose in his Shepherdess's Hair," were to see a mightier change than the usurpation of Louis the Fourteenth's pompous age by the elegant years of Louis the

Fifteenth. But this was not as yet. Here at least we see Boucher's art rid of all outside influences, and at the full tide of creation; here we have the inimitable lightness of touch, the figures and landscape bathed in the airy volume of atmosphere.

He seems at this time to have played with pastel, due probably to his friendship with Latour, who sent a portrait of Boucher's wife to this Salon. Boucher showed in the use of chalks the artistry and skill that were always at his command.

He also was putting to its full use his innate sense of landscape, raising to high achievement that astonishing balance of landscape and figures in his design – a balance that has never been surpassed; his figures never override his landscape; his landscape never overpowers his figures. His earnest counsels to his pupils and his constant deploring of the lack of the landscape art in France prove the great stress he laid upon it.

The designing of a frontispiece for the catalogue of a personal friend, one Gersaint, a merchant of oriental wares, started Boucher in his thirty-third year upon that series of Chinese pictures and tapestries known as the "Chinoiseries," in which he frittered away only too many precious hours, for they were received with great favour by the public. The paintings of Chinese subjects designed for the looms of Beauvais are still to be seen at Besançon.

But busy as were his brain and hand in the exercise of his wide and versatile gifts, pouring out "Chinoiseries," illustrations for books, tapestries on a large scale, landscapes, models for the gilt bronze decorations of porcelain vases, scheming handsome frames for his pictures, designing furniture and fans – Boucher was true, above all, "to his goddess," and painted the famed "Birth of Venus," which, thanks to the Swedish Ambassador's fondness for Madame Boucher, now hangs at Stockholm; our amorous Count de Tessin, to be just, seems to have had a rare flair for the artistic – besides artist's wives. It was on the 15th of April in 1742, the last year of his thirties, that the Royal favour was marked by the grant of a pension of 400 livres (double florins) to Boucher with promise of early benefits to follow. Two years afterwards it was raised to 600 livres.

This was the year that he painted the beautiful canvas of "Diana leaving the Bath with one of her Companions," now at the Louvre. It was also the year that saw his landscape, the "Hamlet of Issé" at the Salon. This "Hameau d'Issé" was to be enlarged for the Opera, proving him to be decorator there, where he was arranging waterfalls, cascades, and the rest of the pretty business, without staying his hand from his art.

At forty Boucher has come into his kingdom. The ten years of these forties were to be a vast triumph for him. He was to produce masterpiece after masterpiece. His art had caught the taste of the day. He was at the height of his powers. He had done great things – he was to do greater. During these ten years of his forties he poured forth vivid and glowing works of sustained power and originality.

We have a picture of him as he was in the flesh at this time – the pastel portrait by Lundberg, now at the Louvre – a gay, somewhat dissipated, handsomely dressed dandy of the time, smiling out of his careless day, the debonnair man of fashion, the laughing eyes showing signs of the night carousals, which were the rest from the prodigious toil of this vital and forthright spirit.

It was in this our artist's fortieth year that the gifted old Cardinal Fleury, who had guided the fortunes of France with rare skill, died, broken by his ninety years and the blunders of the disastrous war that he had so strenuously opposed; and Louis, essaying the strut of kingship, became king by act. His indolent character, unequal to the mighty business, his indeterminate will fretted by the set of quarrelling and intriguing rogues that he gathered about him as his ministers, he fell into the habit that became his thenceforth, the only thing to which he paid the tribute of constancy – he ruled France from behind pretty petticoats. He had early shown the adulterous blood of his great-grandfather; two, if not three, of five sisters of the noble and historic house of De Nesle had yielded to his gadding fancy; the youngest now ousted her sister De Mailly from the king's favour, was publicly acknowledged as the king's mistress, and became Duchess of Châteauroux. Boucher painted her handsome being as a shepherdess in one of his pastorals. She was no ordinary toy of a king. A woman of talent, with hot ambitions for the king's majesty, fired with the pride of race of the old French noblesse, it was during her short years of ascendancy over the king that he roused from his body's torpor and made an effort to reach the dignity and eminence befitting to the lord of a great and gallant people. He stepped forth awhile from his drunken bouts and manifold mean adulteries, and set himself at the head of the army in Flanders, and strutted it as conqueror. Poor Châteauroux only got the hate of the people for reward, Louis the honours; for the people resented the public dishonour of her state. Power she found to be a dead-sea apple in her pretty mouth. The glory of it all, the splendours, were not the easily won delights for which she had looked. She had to fight a duel, that never ended, with the king's witty, crafty, and scurrilous Prime Minister, the notorious Maurepas – and Maurepas willed that no woman should ever come between him and the king – Maurepas who knew no mercy, no decency, no chivalry, no scruple. At Châteauroux's urging, Louis placed himself at the head of the army; and France went near mad with joy that she had again found a king. Crafty Maurepas urged on the business; the Châteauroux suddenly realised his cunning glee – it separated her from the king.

Out of the whirl of things Boucher's fortune was ripening, little as he might suspect it.

He was painting masterpieces that make his name live. To his fortieth year belong the famed "Birth of Venus," the "Venus leaving the Bath," the "Muse Clio," the "Muse Melpomene," and the three well-known pastorals now at the Louvre – "The Sleeping Shepherdess," the "Nest," and the "Shepherd and Shepherd-esses." Of the many famous Venus-pieces that his hand painted during these years it is not easy to write the list. But having signed the "Marriage of Love and Psyche" at forty-one, he turned his experimental hand to the homely, realistic Dutch style that was having a wide vogue, and painted the "Dejeuner" – a family of the prosperous class of the day at breakfast – showing with rare charm the surroundings and home life of the well-to-do of his time.

All goes well with Boucher. He changes into better quarters in the Rue de Grenelle-Saint-Honoré, where he lived for the next five years, until 1749; but his eyes are fixed upon a studio and apartments at the old palace of the Louvre, though the hard intriguing of his powerful friends at Court on his behalf failed for some time. He had, indeed, to make another move before he arrived at his longed-for goal. Pensions Boucher, like others, had found to be somewhat empty affairs; but rooms at the Louvre were a solid possession eagerly sought after by the artists.

In this year of 1744 Boucher created a new fashion at the annual Salon by sending studies and sketches instead of finished pictures; and it set a value upon such things not before realised by artists, for success was instant and loud.

Towards the end of the next, Boucher's forty-second year, the Swedish Ambassador, Count de Tessin, who was to take his leave of Paris, commissioned four pictures to represent the day of a woman of fashion, and to be entitled "Morning," "Midday," "Evening," and "Night." Boucher painted one of these for him, now known as the "Marchande de Modes." The others were painted later, and all had a wide vogue as engravings. The correspondence has interest since it reveals Boucher's business habits; he was paid for a picture on its delivery, and for each of these he was to receive 600 livres (double florins or dollars) – about a hundred and twenty pounds.

In an official document of the Director of Buildings to the king (or Minister of Fine Art, as we should say), written in this year of 1745, Boucher being forty-two, is a "list of the best painters," in which Boucher is singled out for distinction as "an historic painter, living in the Rue de Grenelle-Saint-Honoré, opposite the Rue des Deux-Ecus, pupil of Lemoyne, excelling also in landscape, grotesques, and ornaments in the manner of Watteau; and equally skilled in painting flowers, fruit, architecture, and subjects of gallantry and of fashion."

Not so bad for dry officialdom; the critics could learn a lesson. For he was nothing less. What indeed does he not do? and wondrous well! this painter of the age.

And the mighty rush of events is about to sweep him into further prominence; the very things which he probably passed by with a gay shrug are to enrich him, to help him to his highest fulfilment.

Poor Châteauroux saw that she must lose the king's gadding favour in the conflict with Maurepas unless she joined her lord, now with the army. She realised full well that she had created the new Louis of Ambition – that her going must bring the people's hate to her. But she dared not lose the king. And she went. Maurepas had overdone his jibings. The indiscretion at once rang through the land; became the jest of the army – and Maurepas was not far from the bottom of the business. The discreet indiscretion of covered ways between the king's lodgings and hers only added to the mockeries, and increased the people's hate against, of course, the Châteauroux. Then upon a day in August the small-pox seized Louis at Metz; poor Châteauroux fought for possession of the king in the sick room, until his fear of death – Louis' sole piety – sent her packing – shrinking back in the hired carriage at each halting-place for change of horses, lest she should be seen and torn from her place and destroyed by the populace. But Louis recovered; Paris rang with bells at joy on his recovery, and he entered the city amidst mad enthusiasm, hailed as The Well-Beloved. He sent for the Châteauroux to find her dying, Maurepas having to deliver the message of recall. She died suddenly and in great agony, swearing that Maurepas had poisoned her – died in the arms of her poor discarded sister, the De Mailly.

But this year of 1745 Boucher hears a mightier scandal that is to mean vast things to all France – and not least of all to François Boucher.

VI

THE POMPADOUR

A young bride had become the gossip of the rich merchant society of Paris – that class that was ousting the old noblesse from power. She was a beautiful, a remarkable woman; her wit was repeated in the drawing-rooms, she had all the accomplishments; her charming name – Madame Lenormant d'Etioles.

Draw aside the curtains of the past and we discover our little Jeanne Poisson – grown into this exquisite creature. It has come about in strange fashion enough. The father – a scandalous fellow – having fingered the commissariat moneys in ugly ways to his own use, had been banished for the ugly business. Nor is Jeanne's mother any better than she should be; and the wags wink knowingly at the handsome and rich man of fashion, Monsieur Lenormant de Tournehem, who has been the favoured gallant during the absence of the light-fingered Poisson. And, of a truth, Lenormant de Tournehem takes astonishing interest in the little Jeanne – watching over her up-growing and giving her the best of education at the convent, where she wins all hearts, and is known as "the little queen." The truth spoken with wondrous prophecy, if unthinkingly, as we shall see. Complacent Poisson came home, and took the rich and fashionable, bland and smiling Lenormant de Tournehem to his arms. Has he not wealth and estates? therefore as excellent a friend for Poisson as for Madame Poisson. The girl Jeanne leaves the convent to be taught the accomplishments by the supreme masters of France, the wits foregather at Madame Poisson's, and the brilliant Jeanne is soon mistress of the arts – coquetry not least of all; has also the most exquisite taste in dress. Under all is a heart cold as steel; calculating as the higher mathematics. She has but one hindrance to ambition – her mean birth. Lenormant de Tournehem rids her even of this slur by making his nephew, Lenormant d'Etioles, marry her, giving the young couple half his fortune for dowry, and the promise of the rest when he dies – also he grants him a splendid town-house, as splendid a country seat. And consequential self-respecting little Lenormant d'Etioles is lord of Etioles, amongst other seignories. So Jane Fish appears as Madame Lenormant d'Etioles, seductive, beautiful, accomplished, to whose house repair the new philosophy, the wits, and artists. She has a certain sense of virtue; indeed openly vows that no one but the king shall ever come between her and her lord. But, deep in her heart, she has harboured a fierce ambition – that the king shall help her to keep her bond. She puts forth all her gifts, all her powers, to win to the strange goal; confides it to her worldly mother and "uncle," Lenormant de Tournehem; finds keen allies therein to the reaching of that strange goal. The death of the Châteauroux clears the way. At a masked ball the king is intrigued as to the personality of a beautiful woman who plagues him with her art; he orders the unmasking. Madame Lenormant d'Etioles stands revealed, drops her handkerchief as by accident; the whisper runs through the Court that "the handkerchief has been thrown!" The king stoops and picks it up. A few evenings later she is smuggled into the "private apartments." She goes again a month later; in the morning is seized with sudden terror – she daren't go back to her angry lord lest he do her grievous harm; he will have missed her. The king is touched; allows her to hide from henceforth in the secret apartments; promises the beautiful creature a lodging, her husband's banishment, and early acknowledgment as titular mistress – before the whole Court at Easter, says the pious Great One. But he has to join the army to play the Conqueror at Fontenoy; and it is later in the year (September) before Madame d'Etioles is presented to the Court in a vast company and proceeds to the queen's apartments to kiss hands on appointment. Thus was Jeanne Poisson raised to the great aristocracy of France in her twenty-third year as Marquise de Pompadour.

Boucher had been one of the brilliant group of artists of the d'Etioles' circle. That the Pompadour's influence had much effect upon his position at Court for a year or two is unlikely; for she had to fight for possession of the king day and night, as the Châteauroux had done, against the queen's party and the unscrupulous enmity of Maurepas. To set down Boucher's favour at Court to her is ridiculous. He was painting for the queen's apartments at thirty-one when the Pompadour was a school-girl of twelve. But in the year following her rise to power, Boucher painted four pictures for the large room of the Dauphin, which were "placed elsewhere"; and, the year after that, he was at work upon two pictures for the bedroom of the king at the castle of Marly. It is likely enough that the Pompadour directed this order. She had almost immediately secured the office of the Director-General of Buildings, which covered the direction of the royal art treasures, for "uncle" Lenormant de Tournehem, who was also a friend of the artist. And from this year it is significant that Boucher paints no more for the opposing camp of the Queen and Dauphin.

He was now giving all his strength to the "Rape of Europa" that he painted for the competition ordered by the Academy at the command of Lenormant de Tournehem in the king's name, in which ten chosen Academicians were to paint subjects in their own style for six prizes and a gold medal, to be awarded in secret vote by the competing artists themselves. Boucher won, by his amiable nature, the good-will of them all by proposing that they should so arrange as to share the prizes equally, and thus prevent any sense of soreness inevitable in the losers.

But greatly as he won the good-fellowship of his fellow-artists by it, this picture caused a murmur to rise amongst the critics who, aforetime loud in his praise, now began to complain of his "abuse of rose tints" in the painting of the female nude. The fact was that Diderot and the men of the New Philosophy were turning their eyes to the whole foundations upon which France was built, art as well as society, and were beginning to demand of art "grandeur and morality in its subjects." They were soon to be clamouring for "the statement of a great maxim, a lesson for the spectator." Diderot, with bull-like courage, picked out the greatest, and turned upon Boucher, blaming him for triviality.

The nations, weary of war, concluded the peace of Aix-la-Chapelle in the October of 1748. No sooner was peace concluded than Louis relapsed into his old habit of dandified indolence and profligate ease; and, putting from him his duties as the lord of a great people, he gave himself up to shameless intrigues. He allowed the Pompadour to usurp his magnificence and to rule over the land. He yielded himself utterly, if sometimes sulkily, to her domination; and for sixteen years she was the most powerful person at Court, the greatest force in the state – making and unmaking ministers, disposing of office, honours, titles, pensions. All political affairs were discussed and arranged under her guidance; ministers, ambassadors, generals transacted their business in her stately boudoirs; the whole patronage of the sovereign was dispensed by her pretty hands; the prizes of the Church, of the army, of the magistracy could be obtained solely through her favour and good-will. Her energy must have been prodigious. Possessed of extraordinary talents and exquisite tastes, she gave full rein to them, and it was in the indulgence of her better qualities that Destiny brought Boucher into the friendship of this wonderful woman. She became not only his patron but his pupil, engraving several of his designs.

But this, her sovereignty over the king, easy and light in its outward seeming, was a haggard nightmare to the calculating woman who had so longed for it. She knew no single hour's rest from the night she won to the king's bed. She had to fight her enemies, secret and open, for possession of the king's will, day and night; and she fought – with rare courage. She won by consummate skill and unending pluck. She made herself an essential part of the king's freedom from care. The Court party fought her for power with constant vigilance. Maurepas brought all his unscrupulous art, all his ironic mimicry, all his vile jibes and unchivalrous hatred to bear against her. He had made himself a necessity to the king; and he never slept away a chance of injuring her. He knew no mercy, no nobility, no pity. He made her the detested object of the people. With his own hands he penned the witty verses and epigrams that were sung and flung about the streets of Paris.

But she had an enemy more subtle than any at the Court – hour by hour she had to dispute the king with the king's boredom. And it was in the effort to do so that she created her celebrated theatre in the private apartments, calling Boucher and others to her aid in the doing of it. Here the noblest of France vied with each other to obtain the smallest part to play, an instrument in its orchestra, an invitation to its performances.

Boucher left the Opera to become its decorator in 1748, and did not return until her death. For her, he also decorated her beautiful rooms at Bellevue. She bought at high prices many of his greatest masterpieces.

The Pompadour's power so greatly increased that she openly took command of the king's will; dared and succeeded in getting his favourite Maurepas banished; and herself took to the use of the kingly "we." Her rascally father was created Lord of Marigny; her brother, whom the king liked well and called "little brother," was created Marquis de Vandières; her only child, Alexandrine, signed her name as a princess of the blood royal, and would have been married to the blood royal had she not caught the small-pox and died. She amassed a private fortune, castles, and estates such as no mistress had dreamed of; and into them she poured art treasures that cost the nation thirty-six millions of money. She created the porcelain factory of Sèvres, kept keen watch over the Gobelins looms, and founded the great Military School of St. Cyr amidst work that would have kept several statesmen busy, and of deadly intrigues at Court that would have broken the spirit of many a brilliant man.

It was in her hectic desire to keep the king from being bored that she stooped, and made Boucher stoop, to the employment of his high artistry in the painting of a series of indecent pictures wherewith to tickle the jaded desires of Boredom, and thereby gave rise to the widespread impression that Boucher's art was ever infected by base design. But Boucher was, at his very worst, but a healthy animal; and even in these secret works for the king he did not reach so low as did many an artist of more pious memory who painted with no excuse but his own pleasure.

As a matter of fact, the Pompadour has been blamed too much for this evil act, and too much forgotten for her splendid patronage of the man who, under it and during these great years of his forties, produced a series of masterpieces that place him in the foremost rank of the painters of his century. It is impossible to reckon the number of the pastorals and Venus-pieces that his master-hand painted and loved to paint, during these the supreme years of his genius. It is significant that they were painted during the years that saw the Pompadour in supreme power.

Boucher was so firmly established in 1750, his forty-seventh year, that he moved into a new house in the Rue Richelieu, near the Palais Royal. Disappointed in not receiving a studio and apartments at the Louvre, he was allowed to use a studio in the king's library. He was now making money so easily that he was able to collect pictures and precious stones and the gaily coloured curiosities that appealed to his tastes.

The critics were becoming more and more censorious; and one of them hits true with the comment that in his pastorals his shepherdesses look as if they had stepped over from the Opera and would soon be off again thereto.

In his forty-eighth year Boucher's art was at its most luminous stage – his atmosphere clear and subtle and exquisitely rendered; his yellows golden; his whites satin-like and silvery; his flesh-tones upon the nude bodies of his goddesses unsurpassed by previous art. The beauty of it all was not to last much longer.

Lenormant de Tournehem died suddenly in the November of 1751; the Pompadour's brother, Abel Poisson de Vandières, was appointed Director-General in his stead at the age of twenty-five – and soon afterwards, on the death of his father, created Marquis de Marigny – a shy, handsome youth, a gentleman and an honourable fellow, whom the king liked well, and against whom his sister's sole complaint was that he lacked the brazen effrontery of the courtiers of the day. No man did more for the advancement of the art of his time. A pension of a thousand livres falling vacant, the young fellow secured it for Boucher; and almost immediately afterwards, a studio becoming vacant at the Louvre owing to the death of Coypel, first painter to the king, Boucher came to his coveted home, eagerly moving in with his family as soon as its wretched state could be put into repair.

The decoration of the new wing to the palace at Fontainebleau brought the commission for the painting of the ceiling and the principal picture in the Council Chamber to Boucher, who had already decorated the Dining-Room. This was the period of his painting the "Rising" and the "Setting of the Sun" for the Pompadour, now in the Watteau collection, two canvases that were always favourites with the painter, bitterly as they were assailed by the critic Grimm.

He was turning out so much work that it was impossible to give as much care to his pictures as he ought. For he refused sternly, his life long, to raise his prices; by consequence he had to create a larger amount of work in order to meet his expenditure. It was about this time that Reynolds, passing through Paris, went to visit him and found him painting on a huge canvas without models or sketches. "On expressing my surprise," writes

Reynolds, "he replied that he had considered the model as necessary during his youth until he had completed his study of art, but that he had not used one for a long time past."

He soon had not the time, not only to paint from nature but even to give his pictures the work necessary to complete them. The feverish haste which took possession of him in his frantic endeavour to meet the vast demand for his pictures, and the eager efforts of his engravers to satisfy the public call for engravings after his works, gave him less and less leisure to joy in their doing. And his eyesight began to fail. His flesh-tints deepened to a reddish hue; and he stands baffled before his work, suspecting his sight, since what every one cries out upon as being bright vermilion, he only sees as a dull earthy colour. Boucher has topped the height of his achievement; he has to "descend the other side of the hill." Boucher begins to grow old.

In Boucher's fifty-first year an ugly intrigue of the queen's party at Court to sap the Pompadour's influence over the king by drawing away the king's affections towards Madame de Choiseul-Romanet, a reckless young beauty of the Court, brought about a strange alliance. The Count de Stainville, one of the Pompadour's bitterest enemies, was shown the king's letter of invitation to his young kinswoman; and he, deeply wounded in his pride that his kinswoman should have been offered to the king, went to the Pompadour and exposed the plot. A close alliance followed; and De Stainville thenceforth became her chief guide in affairs of state. It was at her instance that the king called him to be his Prime Minister, raising him to the Duchy of Choiseul – a name he made illustrious as one of the greatest Ministers of France.

In his fifty-second year Boucher was appointed to the directorship of the Gobelins looms, to the huge delight of the weavers and all concerned with the tapestry factory. This was the year of his painting the famous portrait of the Pompadour, to whom he several times paid this "tribute of immorality." For the Gobelins looms he produced many handsome designs; and he was painting with astounding industry. But his hand's skill began to falter. His art shows weariness in his sixtieth year, and sickness fell upon him, and held him in servitude now with rare moments of respite. The critics, notoriously Diderot, were now attacking him with shameless virulence. Boucher passed it all by; but he felt the change that was taking place in the public taste. The ideas of the New Philosophy were infecting public opinion; the Man of Feeling had arisen in the land; and France, humiliated in war, and resenting the follies and the greed of her shameless privileged class, was openly resenting it and all its works. Choiseul had planted his strength deep in the people's party, and was come near to being its god. His masterly mind had checked Frederick of Prussia to the North; and the nations, exhausted by the struggle, signed the Peace of Paris in 1763. Choiseul, with France at peace abroad, turned to the blotting out of the turbulent order of the Jesuits at home. Their attempt to end the Pompadour's relations with the king made this powerful woman eager to complete his design; the chance was soon to come, and the Order was abolished from France and its vast property seized by the state.

The Pompadour lived but a short while to enjoy her triumph. Worn out by her superhuman activities, assailed by debt, she fell ill of a racking cough, dying on the 15th of April, 1764, in her forty-second year, keeping her ascendancy over the king and the supreme power in France to her last hour. Death found her transacting affairs of state. Louis, weary of his servitude, had only a heartless epigram to cast at the body of the dead woman as she passed to her last resting-place.

VII

THE END

The death of the Pompadour robbed Boucher of a friend; but her brother, Marigny, remained faithfully attached to the old artist, and seized every chance to honour him. On the death of Carle van Loo, Boucher, at sixty-two, was made first painter to the king, with all his pensions and privileges that were consistent with this the supreme appointment in the art world.

There had been serious intention of making Boucher the head of the Ecole des Elèves Protegés; he had the art of making himself liked and of inspiring the love of the arts. He was very popular with the students and artists, owing to his kindliness, his eagerness to render service, his readiness to encourage the youngsters or to console them. When the riot took place, provoked by the Academicians by their award of the Prix de Rome in 1767, the students insulted the Academicians, but hailed Boucher with enthusiastic applause. The reason was not far to seek. When a student came to the old master for advice he did not "play the pontiff," and, scorning the false dignity of big phrases, he took the brush in his hand and showed the way out of all difficulties by simplehearted example, despising rules, and putting himself out in order to make things clear to a young artist.

However, the Academicians feared he would be an unorthodox master for youth, and appointed another in his place.

A long and serious illness thwarted his keen energies. Diderot was giving himself up to outrageous violence against him. If the old painter exhibited at the Salon, Diderot fiercely assailed his art; if he did not exhibit, Diderot as bitterly assailed him for his negligences. Above all, he attacked Boucher in that he did not paint what Diderot would have painted – but could not. "When he paints infants," cries Diderot, "you will not find one employed in a real act of life – studying his lesson, reading, writing, stripping hemp."

Poor unfortunate infants! for whom Philosophy could find no happier joy in life than *stripping hemp*! Boucher was but an artist. He painted his generation as far as he could see it, and, with all his faults and weaknesses, he never debauched his art with foreign and alien things that had no part in the nation's life; he painted fair France into his landscapes, not a make-believe land he did not know with preposterous Greek ruins; and best of all, to his eternal honour, he painted infants glad in their gladness to be alive, with no desire to send their happy little bodies to school, with no sickly ambition to make them into budding philosophers, with no thought of making them pose and lie as Men of Feeling. He had no joy in setting their little bodies to toil – in making them "teach a lesson to the spectator," in making them stoop their little shoulders to the "picking of hemp."

He continued to paint as he had always painted – except that he painted less well. The wreath of roses was wilting on a grey head. The blood jigged less warmly in the frail body. The features showed pallid – the eyes haggard. The sight failed. The hand alone kept something of its cunning.

He went to Holland with his friend Randon du Boisset, but health shrank farther from him. Diderot had near spent his last jibe.

In 1768, Boucher's sixty-fifth year, the neglected queen went to her grave. The king's grief and contrition and vows to amend his life came too late, and lasted little longer than the drying of the floods of tears over the body of his dead consort. A year later he was become the creature of a pretty woman of the gutters, whom he caused to be married to the Count du Barry – the infamously famous Madame du Barry.

But neither the remonstrances of Choiseul with the king against this further degradation of the throne of France, nor his unconcealed scorn of the upstart countess, nor the dangerous enemy he made for himself thereby, signified now to Boucher, first painter to the king.

Boucher was failing. His son was a prig and a disappointment. His two favourite pupils, Baudoin and Deshayes, who had married his two girls, died.

To the Salon of 1769 he sent his "Caravan of Bohemians." It was his last display. He had been going about for some time like a gaunt ghost of his former self, afflicted with all the ills inevitable to a life feverishly consumed in work and the pursuit of pleasure.

They went to his studio at five of the clock one May morning, and found him seated at his easel, before a canvas of Venus, dead, with the paint-filled brush fallen out of his fingers.

So passed he away on the 30th of May 1770, in his sixty-seventh year.

When Boucher died, the generation of which he was the limner was near come to its violent end. The rosy carnivals and gay gallantries of his age gave way to the blood-stained romance and fierce tempest of the Revolution. The garrets of the old curiosity-shops received the discarded canvases of the master. His shepherds and shepherdesses were put to rout by the Romans of his pupil, citizen David. The old order was brought into contempt and overthrown. And with it, Boucher's art, like much that was gracious and charming and good in the evil thing, went down also, and was overwhelmed for a while.

For a while only. For just as, out of the blood and terror of the Revolution, a real France arose, phœnix-wise, from the ruin, and in being born, whilst putting off the vilenesses of the thing from which she sprang, took on also to herself the gracious and winsome qualities that place her amongst the most fascinating peoples of the ages; so Boucher has come into his kingdom again – the most gracious of painters that the years have yielded.

On the following pages are some contemporaries of Boucher.

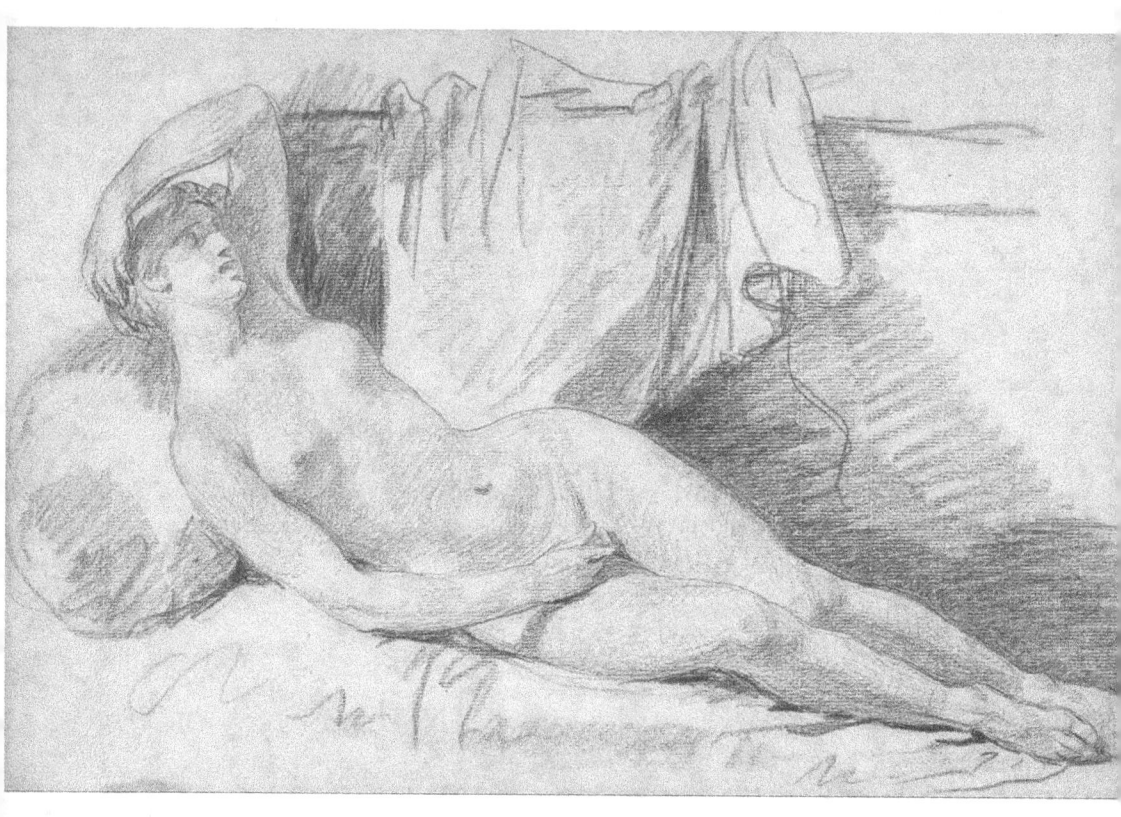

Jean-Baptiste Greuze, Reclining Female Nude,
Study For Aegina Visited By Jupiter, 1762-82

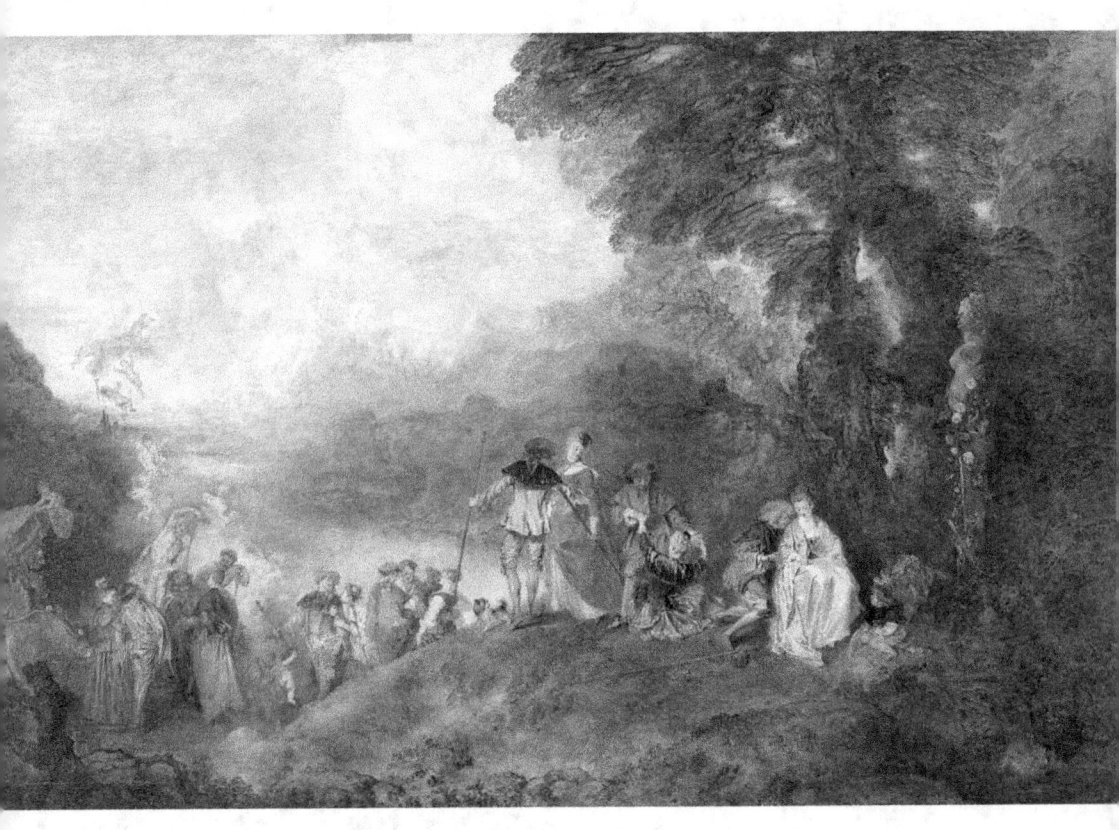

Jean-Antoine Watteau, L'Embarquement pour l'Ile de Cythere, 1717, Louvre, Paris

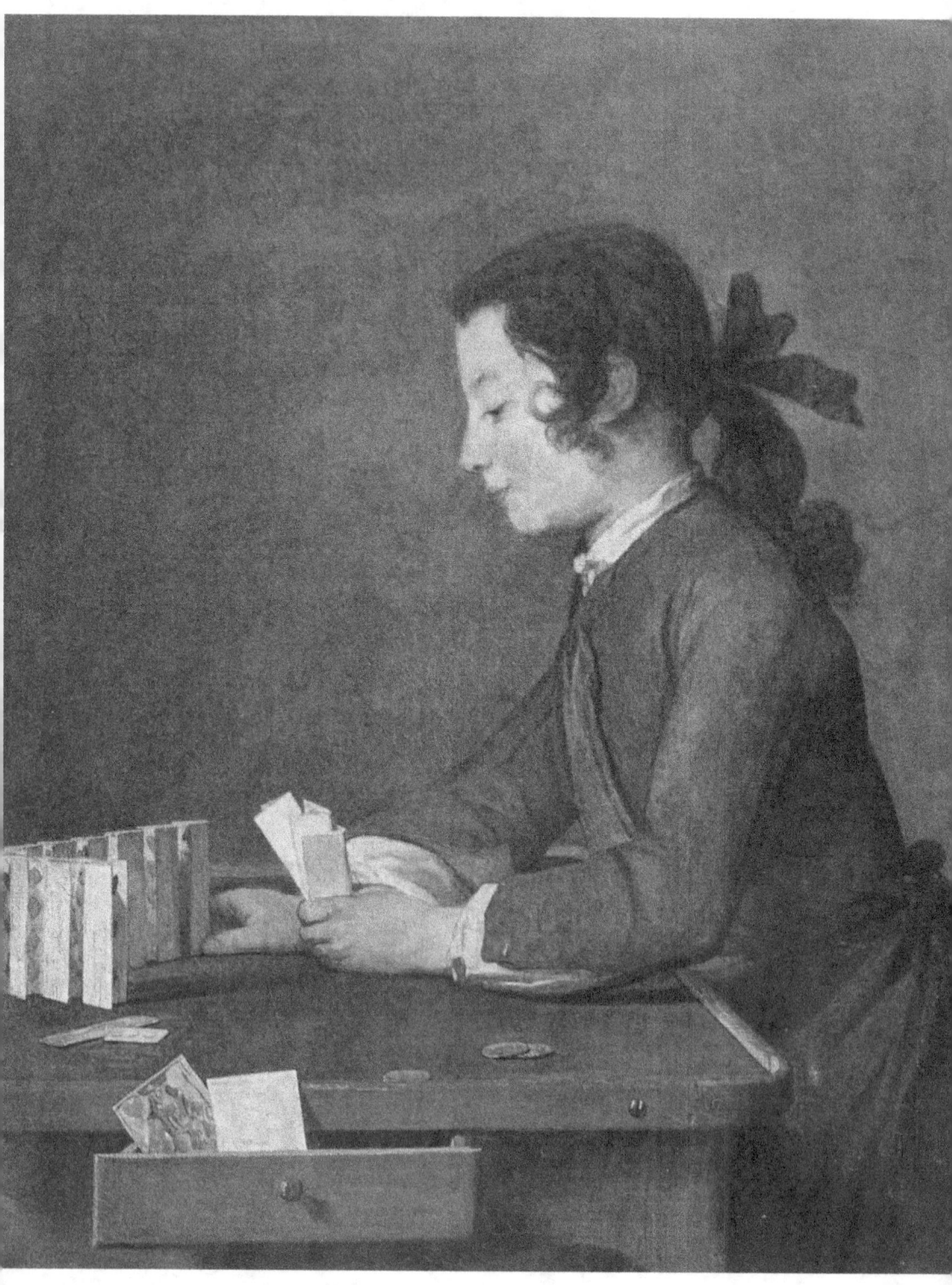

Jean-Baptiste Siméon Chardin, The House of Cards, 1735

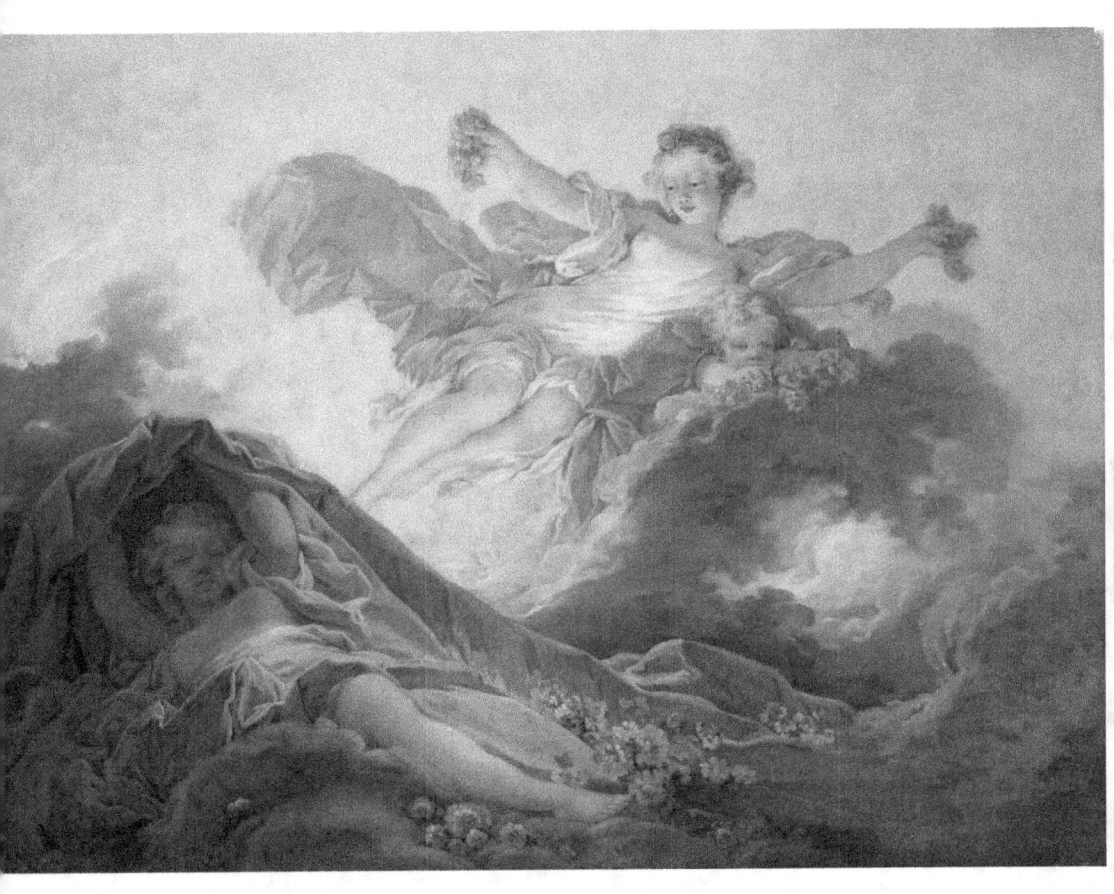

Jean Honoré Fragonard, Aurora, 1775-76

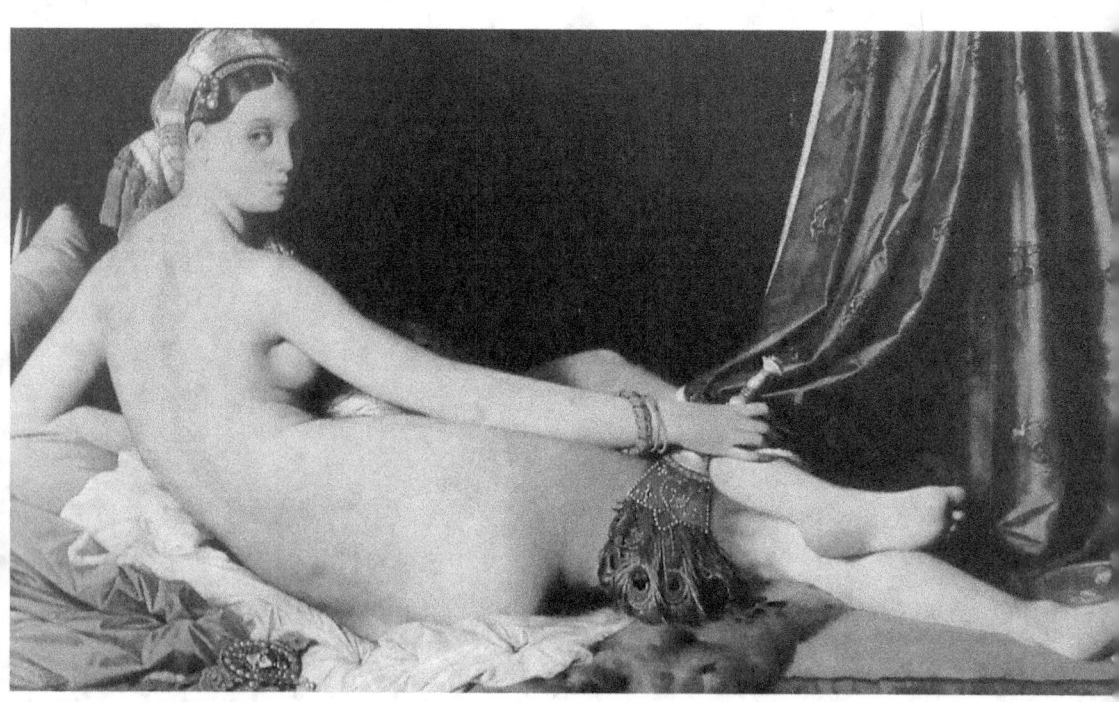

Jean-Dominique Ingres, Grand Odalisque, 1814

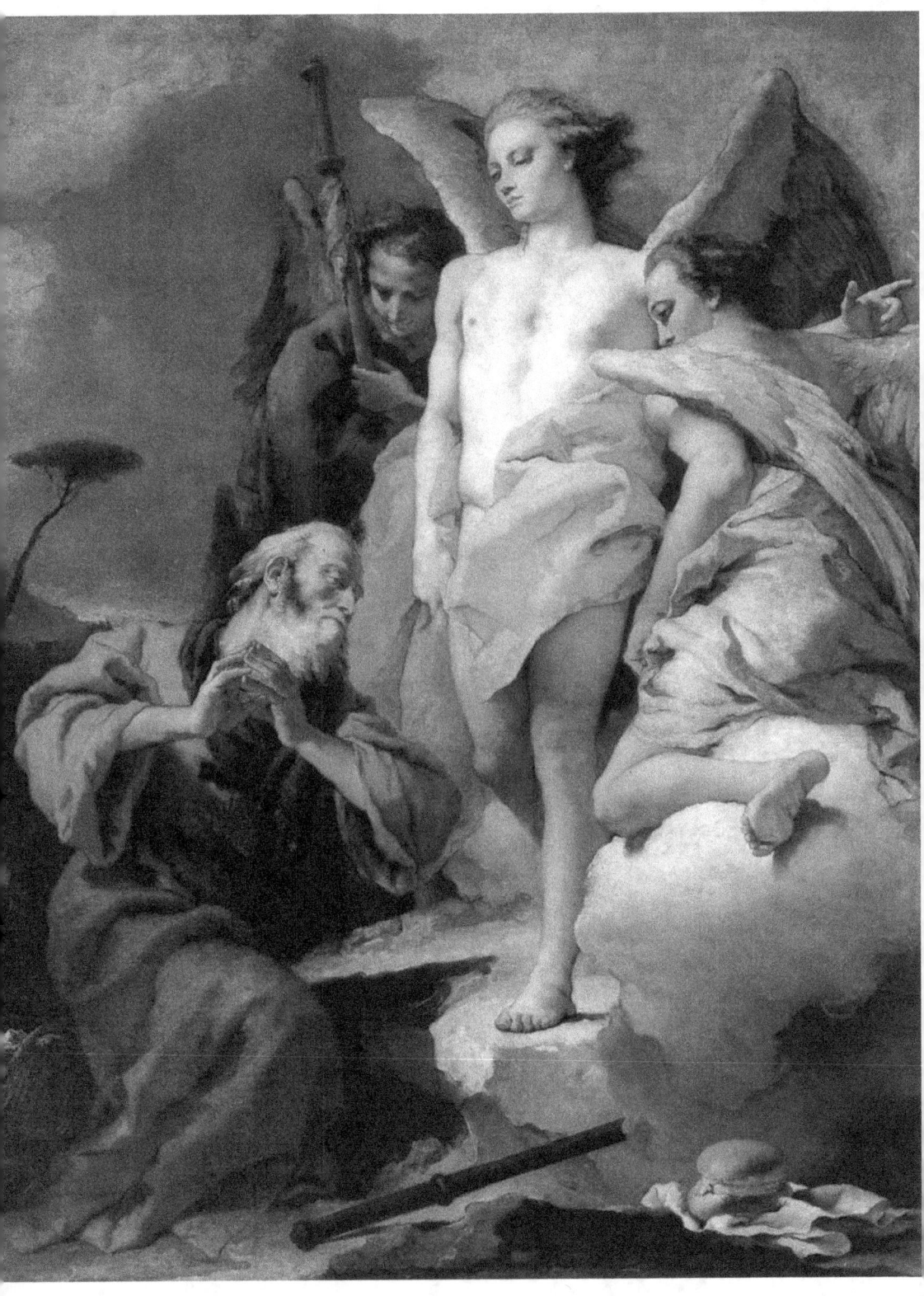

Giovanni Battista Tiepolo, Abraham and Three Angels, c. 1770

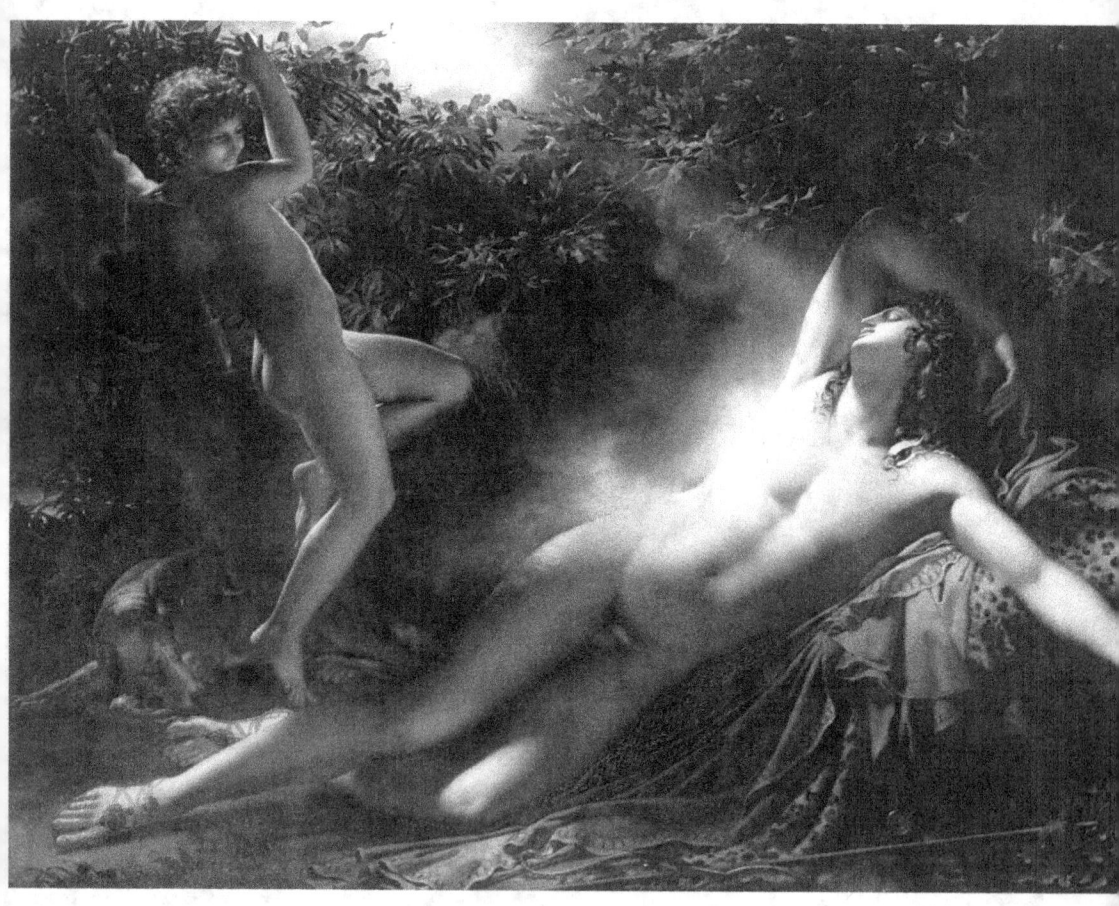

Anne-Louis Girodet-Trioson, Endymion, 1793

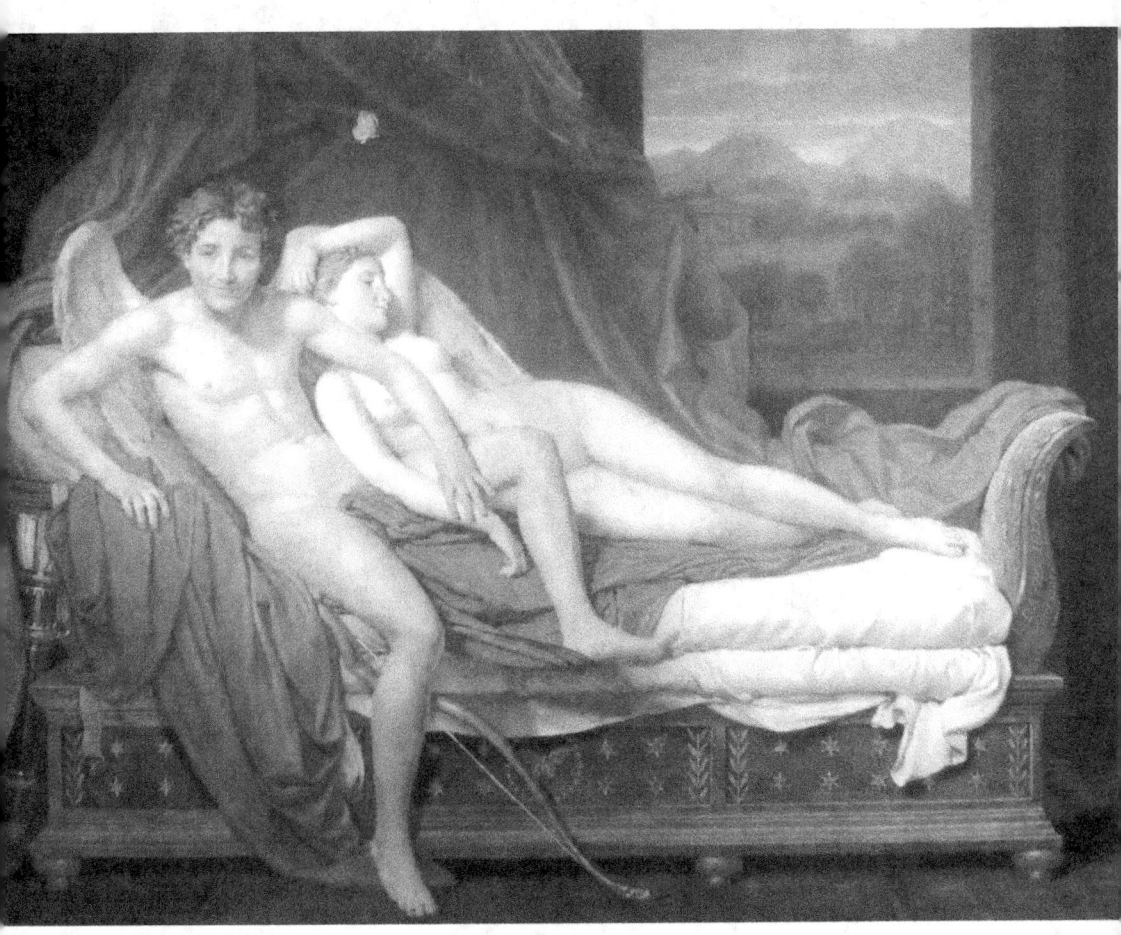

Jacques-Louis David, Cupid and Psyche, 1817,
Cleveland Museum of Art

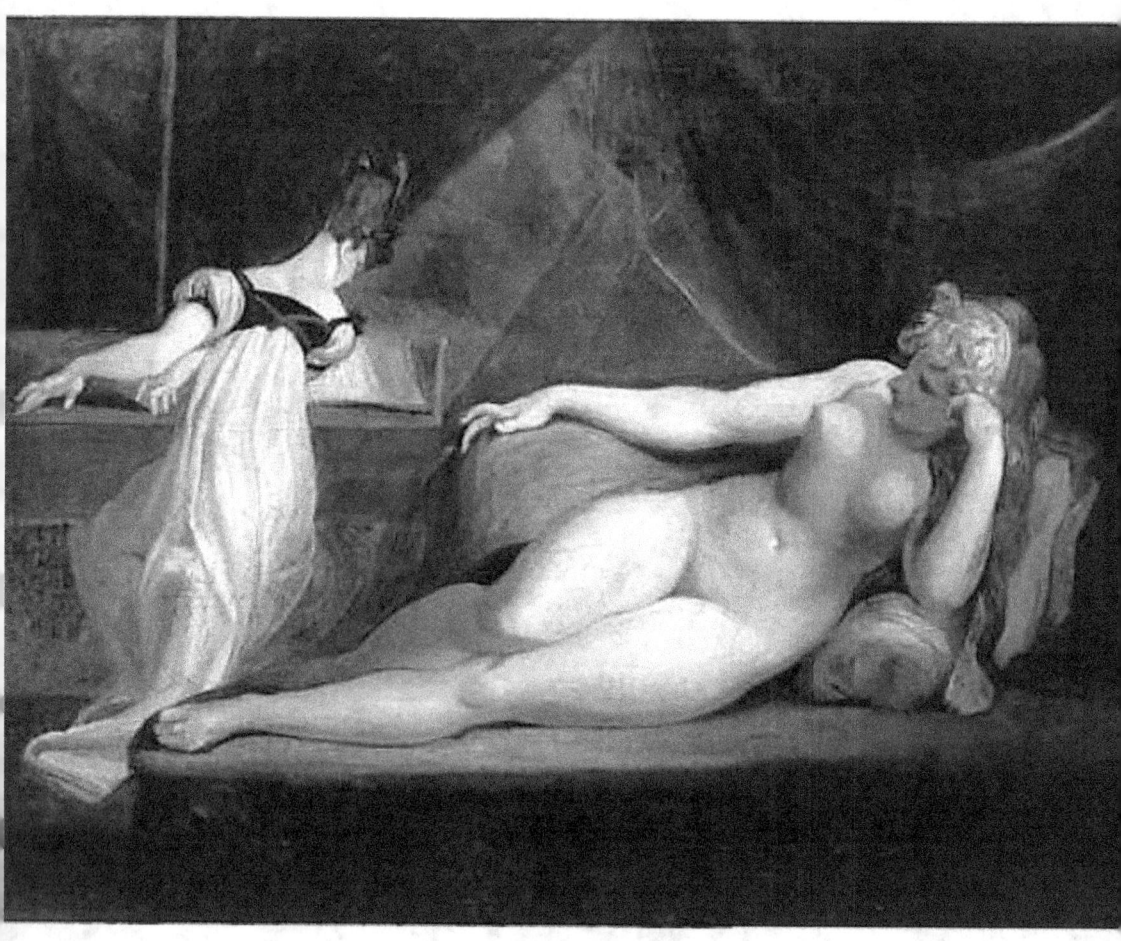

Henry Fuseli

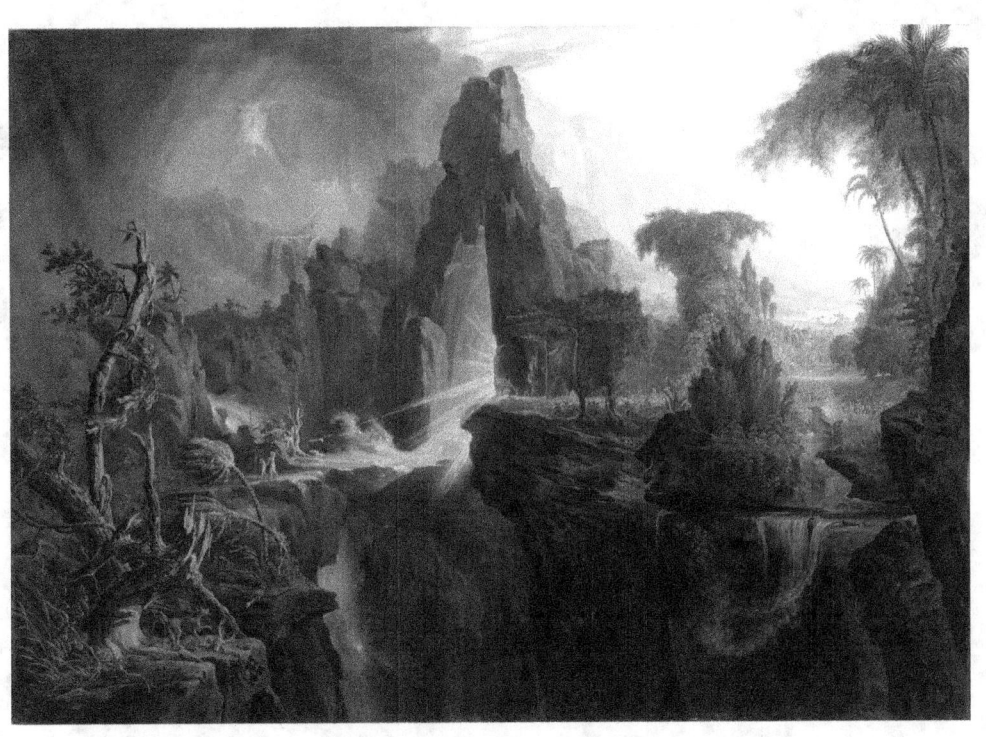

Thomas Cole, Expulsion From the Garden of Eden, 1828,
Museum of Fine Arts, Boston

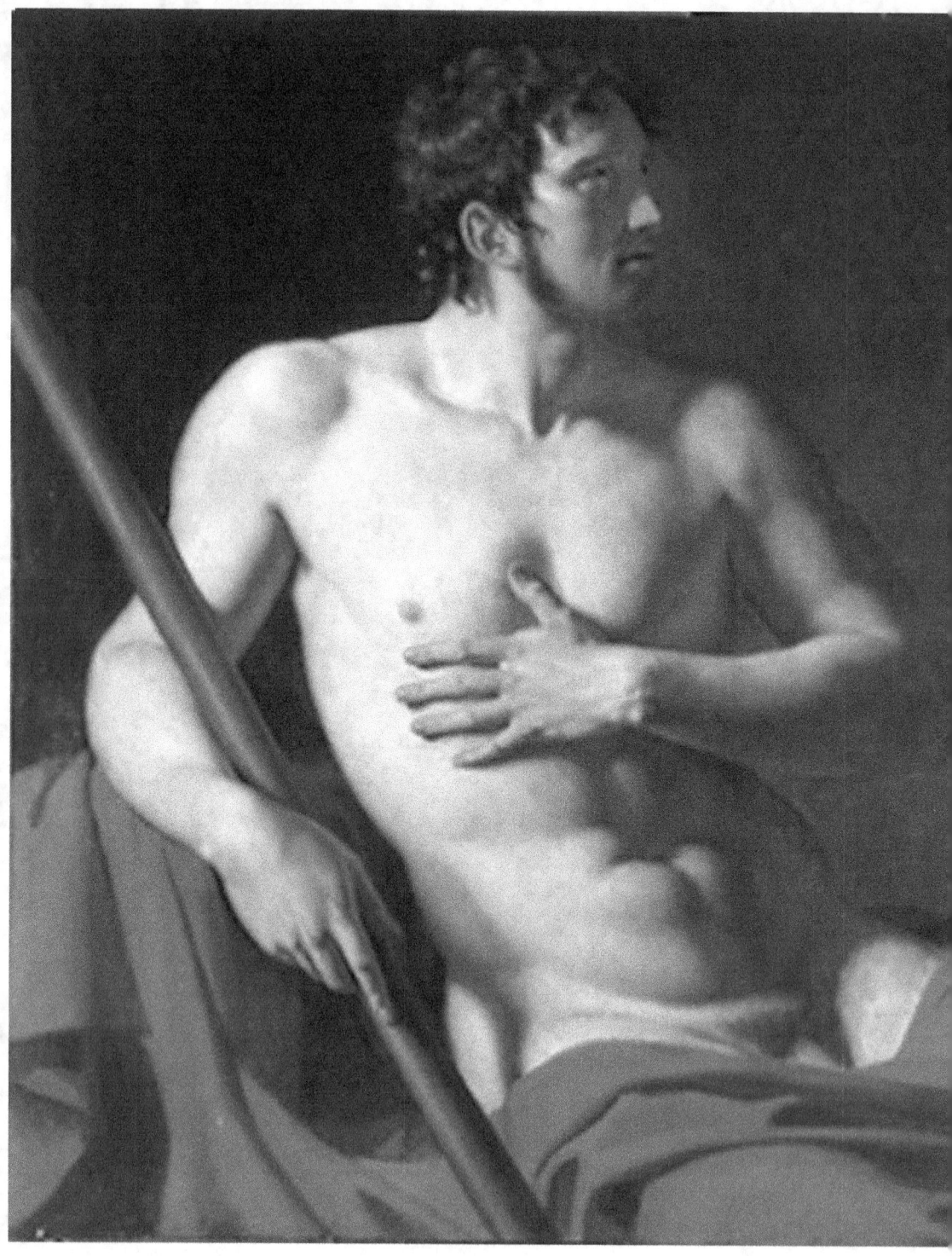

Auguste-Alphonse Gaudar de la Verdine, Male Nude, 1799

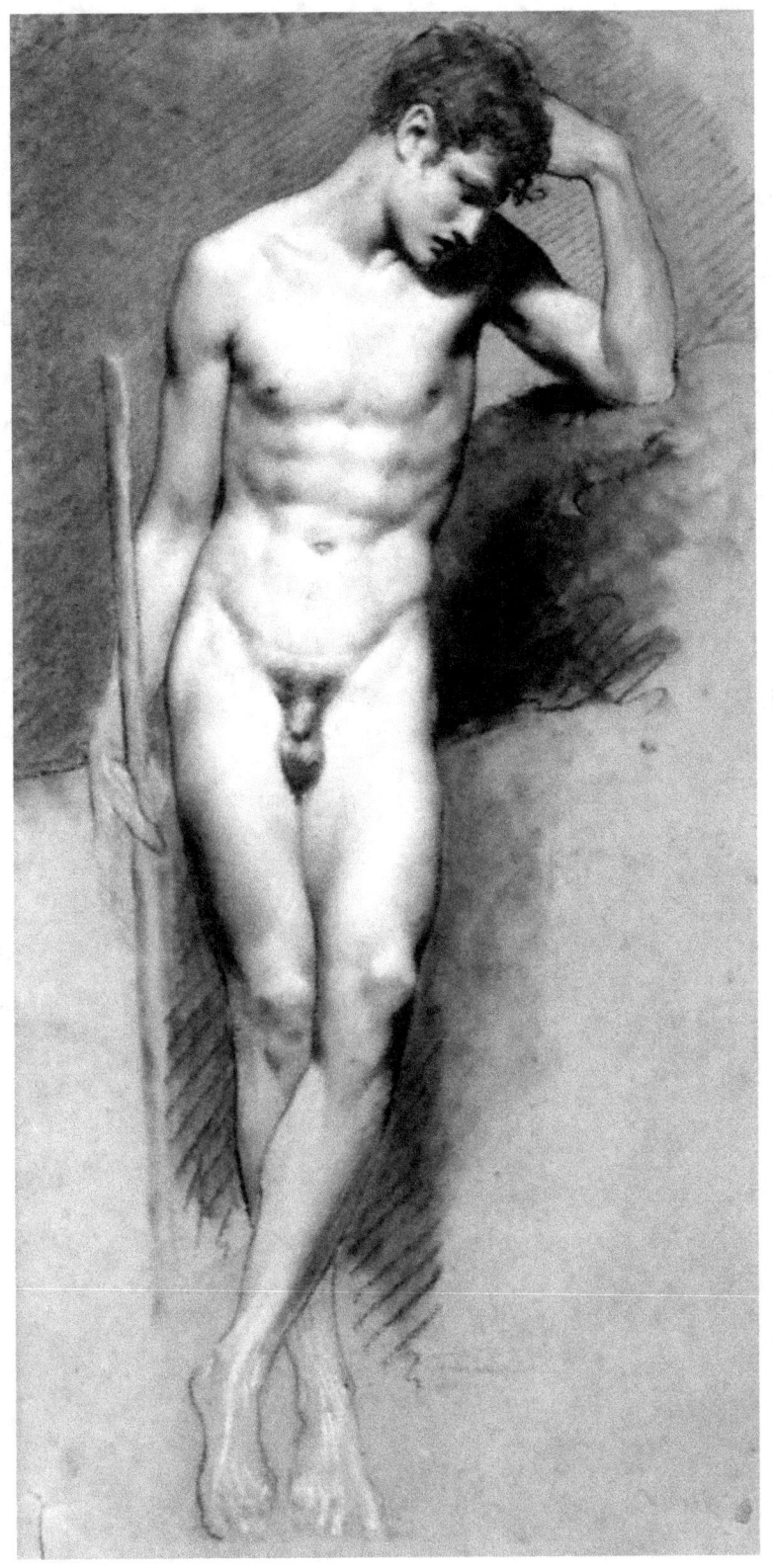

Pierre-Paul Prud'hon (1758-1823), Male Nude Standing

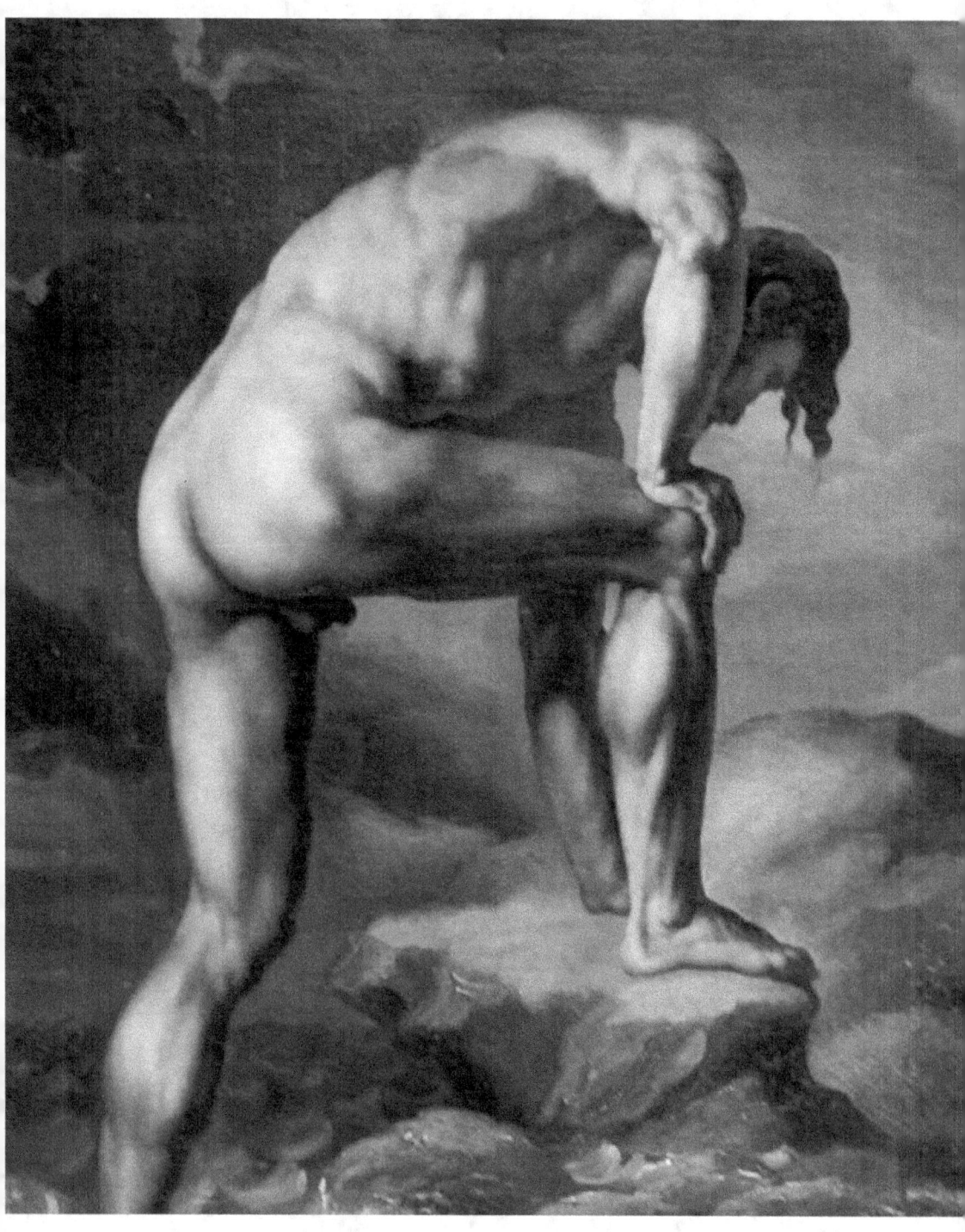

Jean-Louis Andre Theodore Géricault, A Shipwreck, c. 1819

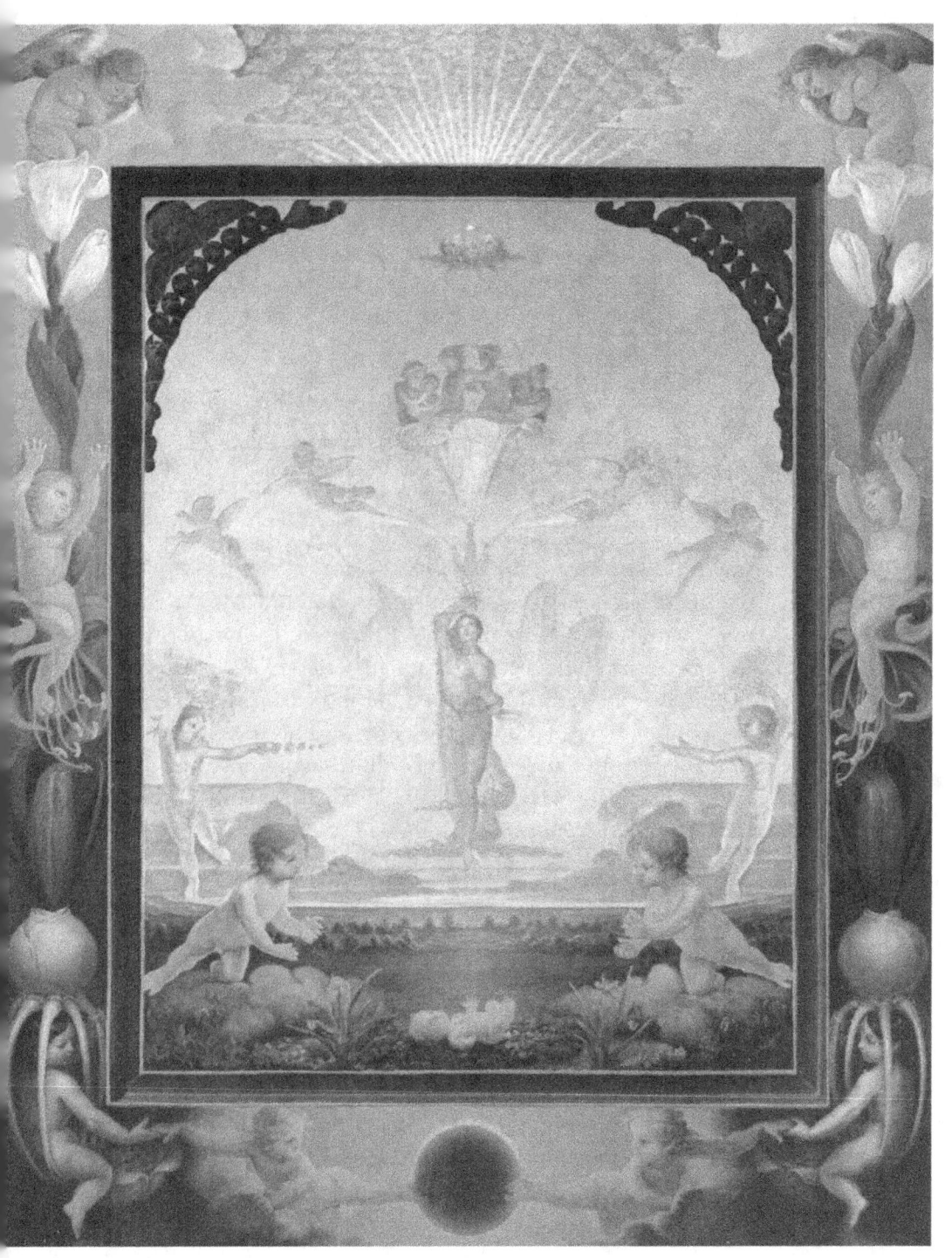

Philipp Otto Runge, Morning, 1808, Hamburg

NOTES ON WORKS

MADAME DE POMPADOUR.
(In the National Gallery of Scotland)

Edinburgh is fortunate in possessing this, one of the world-famous examples of Boucher's exquisite portraiture. He painted with rare charm more than once this wonderful woman, "the king's morsel," Jeanne Poisson, Madame Lenormant d'Etioles, who became the notorious Marquise de Pompadour. He gives us perhaps too dainty a butterfly; for, of a truth, this woman's prettiness masked an iron nerve, an unflinching courage, and a capacity and talents which must have reached to fame in any human being whose frame they illumined. Nor is there hint of those hard qualities that robbed her of mercy, nor allowed her to bend an ear to suffering.

MADAME DE POMPADOUR
(In the Wallace Collection)

Here we have one of the handsomest portraits of his great patron and friend, the notorious Marquise de Pompadour, painted by Boucher at the most brilliant phase of his art. It is a glittering achievement. The figure is superbly placed in its surroundings. The play of limpid light upon the beautifully gowned woman, of which Boucher was such a master-painter, proves it to be of his best period. The Pompadour stands, wreathed in smiles, as the mistress of a great domain; and masks as usual behind her pretty ways all hint of that calculating hand and remorseless will that sent her enemies without a sigh to the Bastille or banishment or worse – she who was past-mistress of the art of the *lettre de cachet*.

DIANA LEAVING THE BATH
(In the Louvre)

The "Diana leaving the Bath with one of her Companions" is amongst the most beautiful of those so-called Venus-pieces that Boucher created and painted in large numbers with decorative intent. It shows his art at its most exquisite stage, when his painting of flesh was at its most luminous and subtle achievement; and his treatment of the human figure in relation to the landscape in which it was placed, at its most perfect balance.

PASTORALE
(In the Louvre)

The "Pastorale," painted a few years after the famous "Diana," also belongs to Boucher's greatest years, and is another of the glories of the Louvre. It is one of his masterpieces in the realm of the Pastoral which he also created – those pleasant landscapes of France in which he places handsomely dressed Dresden shepherds and shepherdesses playing at a dandified comedy of the Simple Life.

PASTORALE
(In the Louvre)

This Pastoral, known as "The Shepherd and Shepherdesses," is another canvas painted at the height of Boucher's career, in which dandified shepherds and shepherdesses seem to have stepped out of the Opera in order to play their light comedy of beribboned simple living in a pleasant landscape of France. It was of these pastorals a waggish critic complained that the shepherds and shepherdesses look as if they must soon be off to the Opera again. But what the carpers omitted was to praise the painting of the pleasant lands of France in which these dainty comedies were set. Boucher has never received his meed of honour as one of the finest landscape-painters of eighteenth-century France.

PORTRAIT OF A YOUNG WOMAN
(In the Louvre)

Of the rare portraits painted by Boucher, it is strange that the sitter to this finely painted canvas is now wholly forgotten. But the picture remains to prove to us the wide range of Boucher's genius.

INTERIEUR DE FAMILLE
(In the Louvre)

Boucher had a quick ear for the vogue. Twice he found the Home to be in the artistic fashion; and each time he painted Home life in order to be in the mode. This interior, showing a well-to-do French family of the times at the midday meal, is not only rendered with glitter and atmosphere, but it is valuable as a rich record of the manners and furnishments of his day.

LA MODISTE
(In the Wallace Collection)

The "Modiste" that now hangs at the Wallace is a slight variation on the "Toilet" that went to Stockholm, commissioned by the Swedish Ambassador as "Morning" (with three others, to represent the Midday, Evening, and Night of a fashionable woman's day, but which were never painted). The "Modiste" or "Morning," was engraved by Gaillard as "La Marchande de Modes," which adds somewhat to the confusion of its title.

MAURICE SENDAK

& the art of children's book illustration

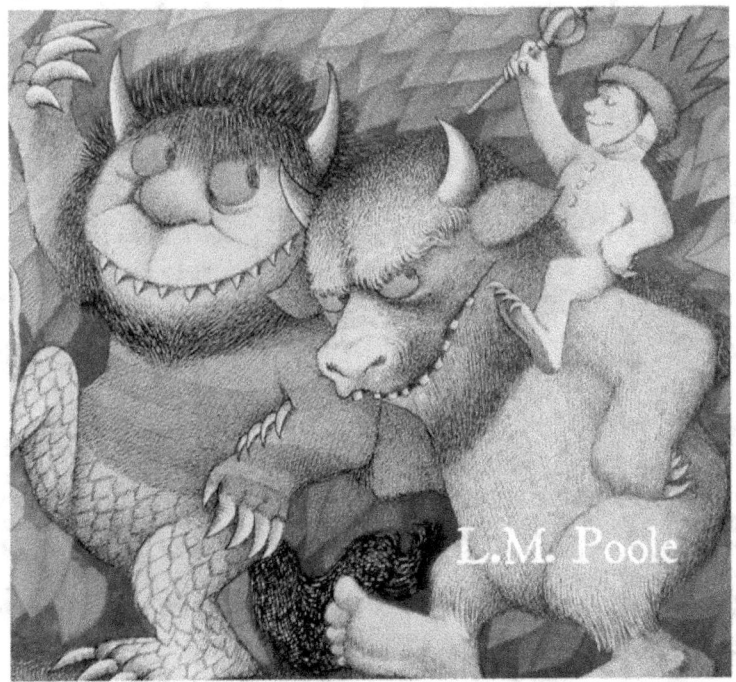

L.M. Poole

Maurice Sendak is the widely acclaimed American children's book author and illustrator. This critical study focuses on his famous trilogy, *Where the Wild Things Are, In the Night Kitchen* and *Outside Over There*, as well as the early works and Sendak's superb depictions of the Grimm Brothers' fairy tales in *The Juniper Tree*. L.M. Poole begins with a chapter on children's book illustration, in particular the treatment of fairy tales. Sendak's work is situated within the history of children's book illustration, and he is compared with many contemporary authors.

Fully illustrated. The book has been revised and updated for this edition.

ISBN 9781861714282 Pbk   ISBN 9781861713469 Hbk

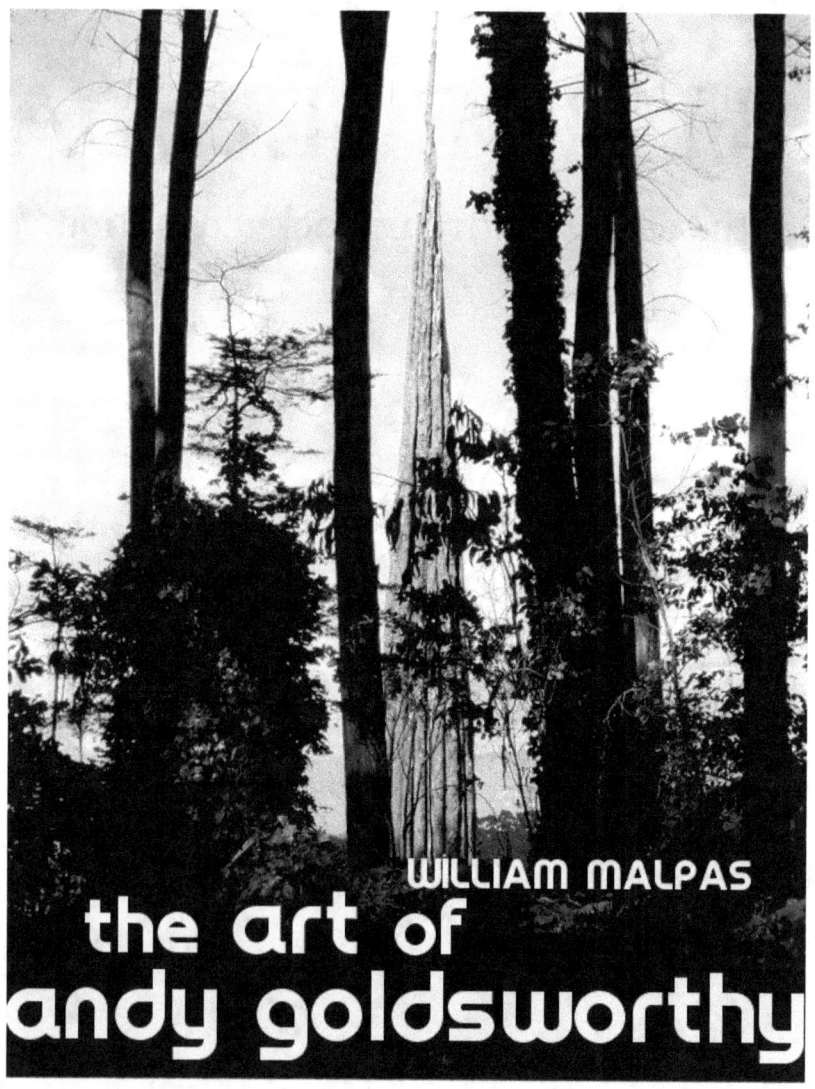

WILLIAM MALPAS

the art of
andy goldsworthy

This is the most comprehensive and detailed account of the art of Andy Goldsworthy available.

This study of Andy Goldsworthy discusses all of Goldsworthy's major exhibitions, books and projects, including the *Sheepfolds* project; *Garden of Stones* in New York; TV and dance collaborations; and the books *Wood, Stone, Time* and *Passage*. William Malpas surveys all of Goldsworthy's output, and analyzes his relation with other land artists such as Robert Smithson, the Christos, Walter de Maria, Chris Drury, Richard Long and David Nash; women sculptors; sculpture in the modern era; and Goldsworthy's place in the contemporary British art scene.

The book has been updated and revised for this new edition.

ISBN 9781861714107 Pbk   ISBN 9781861714114 Hbk
Fully illustrated   www.crmoon.com

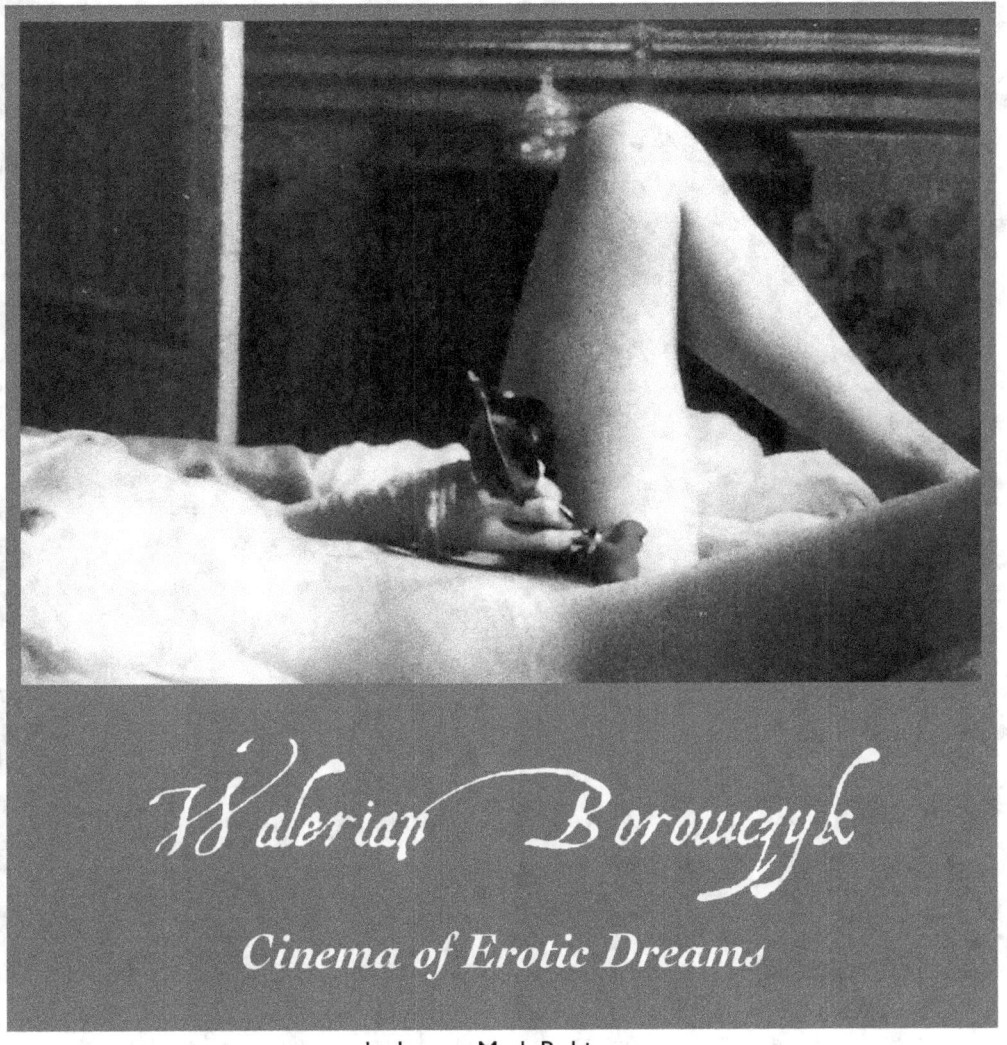

Walerian Borowczyk

Cinema of Erotic Dreams

by Jeremy Mark Robinson

Walerian Borowczyk (1923-2006) was a Polish artist, animator and filmmaker who lived in France for much of his life. He is the author of European art cinema masterpieces *Goto: Island of Love, Blanche* and *Immoral Tales*, some surreal animated shorts, and controversial films such as *The Beast*. This new book concentrates on Borowczyk's feature films, from *Goto* to *Love Rites*, which contain some of the most extraordinary images and scenes in recent cinema. Erotica for some, porn for others, Borowczyk's films are highly idiosyncratic and unforgettable.

Bibliography, notes, 110 illustrations   252pp.
ISBN 9781861713674 Pbk   ISBN 9781861713124 Hbk

Also available: *Walerian Borowczyk: The Beast: Pocket Movie Guide*

Beauties, Beasts, and Enchantment

CLASSIC FRENCH FAIRY TALES

Translated and with an Introduction
by Jack Zipes

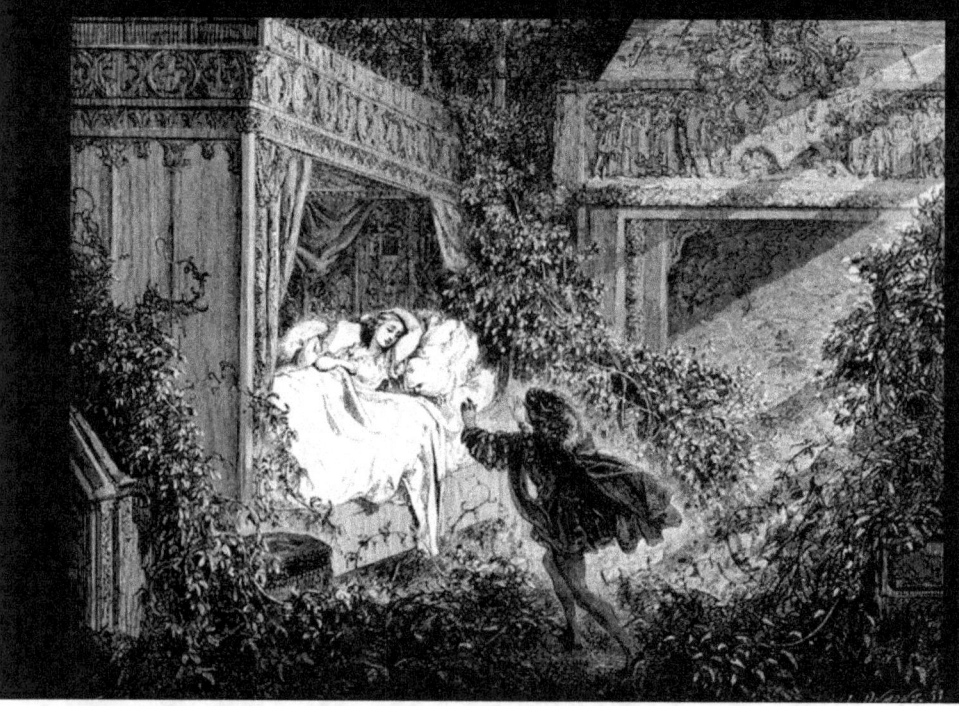

A collection of 36 classic French fairy tales translated by renowned writer Jack Zipes.
Cinderella, Beauty and the Beast, Sleeping Beauty and *Little Red Riding Hood* are among the
classic fairy tales in this amazing book.
Includes illustrations from fairy tale collections.
Jack Zipes has written and published widely on fairy tales.

'Terrific... a succulent array of 17th and 18th century 'salon' fairy tales'
- *The New York Times Book Review*

'These tales are adventurous, thrilling in a way fairy tales are meant to be... The translation
from the French is modern, happily free of archaic and hyperbolic language... a fine and
sophisticated collection' - *New York Tribune*

'Enjoyable to read... a unique collection of French regional folklore' - *Library Journal*

'Charming stories accompanied by attractive pen-and-ink drawings' - *Chattanooga Times*

Introduction and illustrations   612pp.   ISBN 9781861712510 Pbk   ISBN 9781861713193 Hbk

CRESCENT MOON PUBLISHING

web: www.crmoon.com e-mail: cresmopub@yahoo.co.uk

ARTS, PAINTING, SCULPTURE

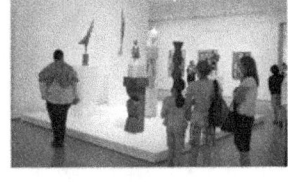
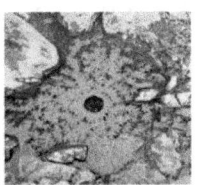
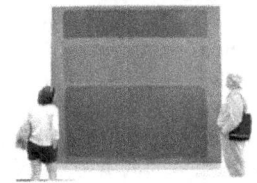

The Art of Andy Goldsworthy
Andy Goldsworthy: Touching Nature
Andy Goldsworthy in Close-Up
Andy Goldsworthy: Pocket Guide
Andy Goldsworthy In America
Land Art: A Complete Guide
The Art of Richard Long
Richard Long: Pocket Guide
Land Art In the UK
Land Art in Close-Up
Land Art In the U.S.A.
Land Art: Pocket Guide
Installation Art in Close-Up
Minimal Art and Artists In the 1960s and After
Colourfield Painting
Land Art DVD, TV documentary
Andy Goldsworthy DVD, TV documentary
The Erotic Object: Sexuality in Sculpture From Prehistory to the Present Day
Sex in Art: Pornography and Pleasure in Painting and Sculpture
Postwar Art
Sacred Gardens: The Garden in Myth, Religion and Art
Glorification: Religious Abstraction in Renaissance and 20th Century Art
Early Netherlandish Painting
Leonardo da Vinci
Piero della Francesca
Giovanni Bellini
Fra Angelico: Art and Religion in the Renaissance
Mark Rothko: The Art of Transcendence
Frank Stella: American Abstract Artist
Jasper Johns
Brice Marden
Alison Wilding: The Embrace of Sculpture
Vincent van Gogh: Visionary Landscapes
Eric Gill: Nuptials of God
Constantin Brancusi: Sculpting the Essence of Things
Max Beckmann
Caravaggio
Gustave Moreau
Egon Schiele: Sex and Death In Purple Stockings
Delizioso Fotografico Fervore: Works In Process 1
Sacro Cuore: Works In Process 2
The Light Eternal: J.M.W. Turner
The Madonna Glorified: Karen Arthurs

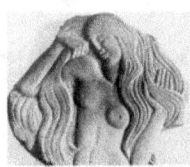
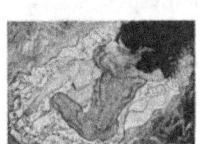
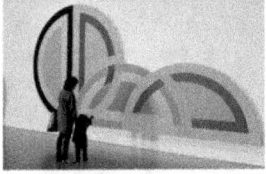
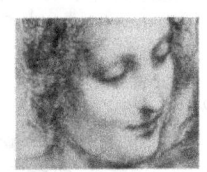
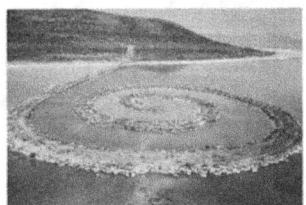

LITERATURE

J.R.R. Tolkien: The Books, The Films, The Whole Cultural Phenomenon
J.R.R. Tolkien: Pocket Guide
Tolkien's Heroic Quest
The *Earthsea* Books of Ursula Le Guin
Beauties, Beasts and Enchantment: Classic French Fairy Tales
German Popular Stories by the Brothers Grimm
Philip Pullman and *His Dark Materials*
Sexing Hardy: Thomas Hardy and Feminism
Thomas Hardy's *Tess of the d'Urbervilles*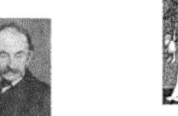
Thomas Hardy's *Jude the Obscure*
Thomas Hardy: The Tragic Novels
Love and Tragedy: Thomas Hardy
The Poetry of Landscape in Hardy
Wessex Revisited: Thomas Hardy and John Cowper Powys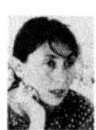
Wolfgang Iser: Essays and Interviews
Petrarch, Dante and the Troubadours
Maurice Sendak and the Art of Children's Book Illustration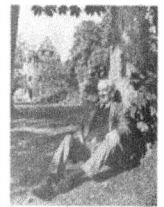
Andrea Dworkin
Cixous, Irigaray, Kristeva: The *Jouissance* of French Feminism
Julia Kristeva: Art, Love, Melancholy, Philosophy, Semiotics and Psychoanalysis
Hélène Cixous I Love You: The *Jouissance* of Writing
Luce Irigaray: Lips, Kissing, and the Politics of Sexual Difference
Peter Redgrove: Here Comes the Flood
Peter Redgrove: Sex-Magic-Poetry-Cornwall
Lawrence Durrell: Between Love and Death, East and West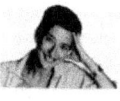
Love, Culture & Poetry: Lawrence Durrell
Cavafy: Anatomy of a Soul
German Romantic Poetry: Goethe, Novalis, Heine, Hölderlin
Feminism and Shakespeare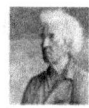
Shakespeare: Love, Poetry & Magic
The Passion of D.H. Lawrence
D.H. Lawrence: Symbolic Landscapes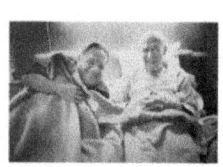
D.H. Lawrence: Infinite Sensual Violence
Rimbaud: Arthur Rimbaud and the Magic of Poetry
The Ecstasies of John Cowper Powys
Sensualism and Mythology: The Wessex Novels of John Cowper Powys
Amorous Life: John Cowper Powys and the Manifestation of Affectivity (H.W. Fawkner)
Postmodern Powys: New Essays on John Cowper Powys (Joe Boulter)
Rethinking Powys: Critical Essays on John Cowper Powys
Paul Bowles & Bernardo Bertolucci
Rainer Maria Rilke
Joseph Conrad: *Heart of Darkness*
In the Dim Void: Samuel Beckett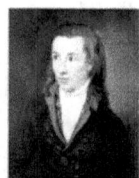
Samuel Beckett Goes into the Silence
André Gide: Fiction and Fervour
Jackie Collins and the Blockbuster Novel
Blinded By Her Light: The Love-Poetry of Robert Graves
The Passion of Colours: Travels In Mediterranean Lands
Poetic Forms

POETRY

Ursula Le Guin: Walking In Cornwall
Peter Redgrove: Here Comes The Flood
Peter Redgrove: Sex-Magic-Poetry-Cornwall
Dante: Selections From the Vita Nuova
Petrarch, Dante and the Troubadours
William Shakespeare: Sonnets
William Shakespeare: Complete Poems
Blinded By Her Light: The Love-Poetry of Robert Graves
Emily Dickinson: Selected Poems
Emily Brontë: Poems
Thomas Hardy: Selected Poems
Percy Bysshe Shelley: Poems
John Keats: Selected Poems
Joh n Keats: Poems of 1820
D.H. Lawrence: Selected Poems
Edmund Spenser: Poems
Edmund Spenser: Amoretti
John Donne: Poems
Henry Vaughan: Poems
Sir Thomas Wyatt: Poems
Robert Herrick: Selected Poems
Rilke: Space, Essence and Angels in the Poetry of Rainer Maria Rilke
Rainer Maria Rilke: Selected Poems
Friedrich Hölderlin: Selected Poems
Arseny Tarkovsky: Selected Poems
Arthur Rimbaud: Selected Poems
Arthur Rimbaud: A Season in Hell
Arthur Rimbaud and the Magic of Poetry
Novalis: Hymns To the Night
German Romantic Poetry
Paul Verlaine: Selected Poems
Elizaethan Sonnet Cycles
D.J. Enright: By-Blows
Jeremy Reed: Brigitte's Blue Heart
Jeremy Reed: Claudia Schiffer's Red Shoes
Gorgeous Little Orpheus
Radiance: New Poems
Crescent Moon Book of Nature Poetry
Crescent Moon Book of Love Poetry
Crescent Moon Book of Mystical Poetry
Crescent Moon Book of Elizabethan Love Poetry
Crescent Moon Book of Metaphysical Poetry
Crescent Moon Book of Romantic Poetry
Pagan America: New American Poetry

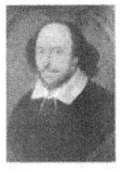
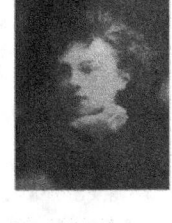
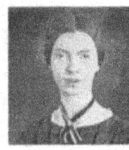
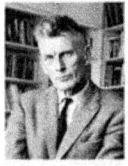
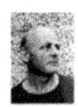
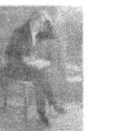
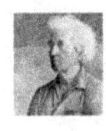
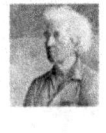
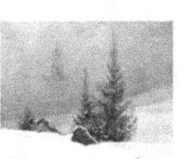
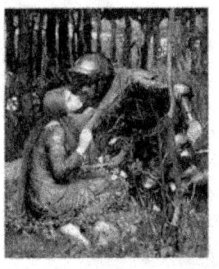
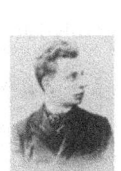
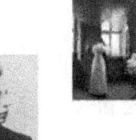
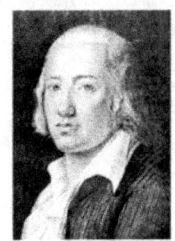
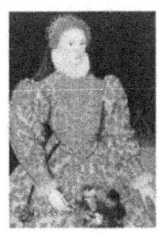

MEDIA, CINEMA, FEMINISM and CULTURAL STUDIES

J.R.R. Tolkien: The Books, The Films, The Whole Cultural Phenomenon
J.R.R. Tolkien: Pocket Guide
The *Lord of the Rings* Movies: Pocket Guide
The Cinema of Hayao Miyazaki
Hayao Miyazaki: *Princess Mononoke*: Pocket Movie Guide
Hayao Miyazaki: *Spirited Away*: Pocket Movie Guide
Tim Burton : Hallowe'en For Hollywood
Ken Russell

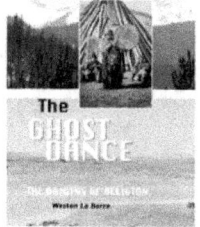

Ken Russell: *Tommy*: Pocket Movie Guide
The Ghost Dance: The Origins of Religion
The Peyote Cult
Cixous, Irigaray, Kristeva: The *Jouissance* of French Feminism
Julia Kristeva: Art, Love, Melancholy, Philosophy, Semiotics and Psychoanalysis
Luce Irigaray: Lips, Kissing, and the Politics of Sexual Difference
Hélene Cixous I Love You: The *Jouissance* of Writing
Andrea Dworkin

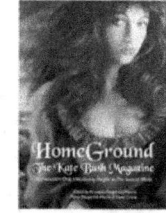

'Cosmo Woman': The World of Women's Magazines
Women in Pop Music
HomeGround: The Kate Bush Anthology
Discovering the Goddess (Geoffrey Ashe)
The Poetry of Cinema

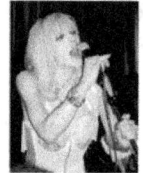

The Sacred Cinema of Andrei Tarkovsky
Andrei Tarkovsky: Pocket Guide
Andrei Tarkovsky: *Mirror*: Pocket Movie Guide
Andrei Tarkovsky: *The Sacrifice*: Pocket Movie Guide
Walerian Borowczyk: Cinema of Erotic Dreams
Jean-Luc Godard: The Passion of Cinema

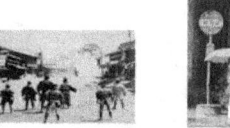

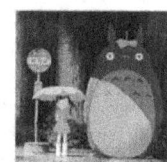

Jean-Luc Godard: *Hail Mary*: Pocket Movie Guide
Jean-Luc Godard: *Contempt*: Pocket Movie Guide
Jean-Luc Godard: *Pierrot le Fou*: Pocket Movie Guide
John Hughes and Eighties Cinema
Ferris Bueller's Day Off: Pocket Movie Guide
Jean-Luc Godard: Pocket Guide
The Cinema of Richard Linklater

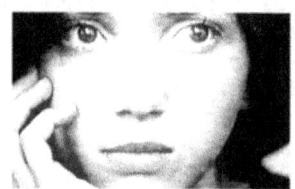

Liv Tyler: Star In Ascendance
Blade Runner and the Films of Philip K. Dick
Paul Bowles and Bernardo Bertolucci
Media Hell: Radio, TV and the Press
An Open Letter to the BBC
Detonation Britain: Nuclear War in the UK
Feminism and Shakespeare
Wild Zones: Pornography, Art and Feminism
Sex in Art: Pornography and Pleasure in Painting and Sculpture
Sexing Hardy: Thomas Hardy and Feminism

The Light Eternal is a model monograph, an exemplary job. The subject matter of the book is beautifully
organised and dead on beam. (Lawrence Durrell)
It is amazing for me to see my work treated with such passion and respect. (Andrea Dworkin)

CRESCENT MOON PUBLISHING
P.O. Box 1312, Maidstone, Kent, ME14 5XU, Great Britain. www.crmoon.com

cresmopub@yahoo.co.uk   www.crescentmoon.org.uk

www.ingramcontent.com/pod-product-compliance
Lightning Source LLC
Chambersburg PA
CBHW051325220526
45468CB00004B/1501